The Focused Faith

Brian Bovee

Published by Brian Bovee, 2024.

While every precaution has been taken in the preparation of this book, the publisher assumes no responsibility for errors or omissions, or for damages resulting from the use of the information contained herein.

THE FOCUSED FAITH

First edition. December 31, 2024.

Copyright © 2024 Brian Bovee.

ISBN: 979-8218513535

Written by Brian Bovee.

Table of Contents

Preface 1

Introduction 7

Lost in Scroll: Why Focus Feels Impossible 15

Flowing into Abundance: The True Cure for a Distracted Mind 35

Screens and Souls: How Technology Shapes Our Walk with God 59

Alone, Not Lonely: The Transformative Gift of Solitude 71

Focused Hearts, Open Souls: Attention and Prayer 85

The Lost Art of Deep Reading: Navigating the Noise to Find Truth 100

Purging Distraction: The Transformative Journey of Detox and Flow 114

Conclusion 134

To God, the Author of all things good and to my wife, Sheila, whose love and support have been my constant strength. May this work reflect the beauty of love and faith that both of you have instilled in me.

Copyright © 2024 by Brian Bovee All rights reserved. No part of this publication may be reproduced, stored or transmitted in any form or by any means, electronic, mechanical, photocopying, recording, scanning, or otherwise without written permission from the publisher. It is illegal to copy this book, post it to a website, or distribute it by any other means without permission. Scripture quotations unless otherwise noted are from the New International Version (NIV). First edition.

Thank you for purchasing *The Focused Faith*! As a special gift, I'd love for you to download the FREE Focused Faith Application Guide. This hands-on resource will help you apply the principles in the book to reclaim your attention and deepen your relationship with God. Don't miss out on this exclusive offer—get your free guide now here[1].

---

1. https://www.thefocusedfaith.com/free

The Focused Faith Application Guide is a hands-on resource designed to help you reclaim your attention, break free from the pull of digital distractions, and deepen your relationship with God. Based on the principles introduced in The Focused Faith, this guide takes you through practical, step-by-step strategies for purging distractions, developing focused prayer, and embracing solitude.

Preface

Imagine this scenario: You have just landed after a long flight to a foreign city, far from home. Exhausted from the journey, you drop your bags into the trunk of your rental car and realize your phone is dead due to a broken charging cable *and* there is no GPS in the car. With no map or directions, you make the unwise decision to attempt to start the hour-long journey to your hotel. You find yourself driving aimlessly through unfamiliar streets, taking wrong turns, backtracking, and growing increasingly frustrated as you try to find your way. The more you wander, the more lost you feel, and the more elusive the safety of your hotel becomes.

This scenario might sound like a travel nightmare, but it's an apt metaphor for how many of us live our lives today. Without a clear sense of direction, without focus, we wander through life aimlessly, responding to the immediate demands or distractions of our digital devices. Just as a journey requires a destination and a map, we also need a clear purpose and focus on our journey if we are to reach our goals and live life abundantly.

The apostle Paul understood this well, as he expressed in Philippians 3:13–14, "Forgetting what is behind and straining toward what is ahead, I press on toward the goal to win the prize for which God has called me heavenward in Christ Jesus" (NIV throughout). Paul's singular focus is on his spiritual journey, pressing on toward the goal, despite the distractions of his day. Paul reminds us here that our path to a full and abundant life in Christ requires a deliberate focus and perseverance, ignoring past and present distractions. In the following verse Paul shifts his perspective from his own testimony to his exhortation for you and me: "All of us, then, who are mature should take such a view of things. And if on some point you think differently, that too God will make clear to you."

Paul is calling us here to adopt his same mindset of pressing on toward the goal. He is graciously reminding us that maturity is not about arriving at spiritual perfection but about having the right attitude toward the journey—an attitude of perseverance and focus. Paul acknowledges that while we all have different perspectives and ways to make the journey, the promise is clear: God will reveal His truth to you in due time if you can keep your eyes focused on the prize.

Yet in today's digital world, it can seem impossible to remain focused on God's calling for our lives or keep focused on anything really. From the moment we wake, our attention easily drifts and bounces as if it is under siege from outside forces designed to draw us away from where we intend to focus our thoughts. Our devices buzz with notifications leading us to the infinite scroll of social media and news feeds—all leading us away from deep and meaningful moments of our life. Yet Jesus said, "I have come that they may have life, and have it to the full" (John 10:10). This promise of an abundant life is not found in the superficial satisfaction that our devices offer but in the richness of our relationship with God, the depth of our connections with others, and the pursuit of our true purpose.

This book is *not* another book on how to develop healthy habits for using digital technologies. The dangers of social media and excessive screentime have been researched and discussed ad nauseam. This *is* a book about (1) the attention economy, a system that works tirelessly against you to capture and sustain your attention, and (2) how you can reclaim your focus. My research, including numerous personal interviews with experts and in-depth studies conducted as part of my academic work, reveals that this situation is not merely a matter of personal willpower. It's actually a carefully crafted assault on your ability to concentrate. At first this may sound a bit like the latest conspiracy theory. But stay with me, and I will make the case, using empirically validated research, along with admissions from those running the companies in the attention economy, that your brain is literally being rewired to make it more difficult for you to concentrate. These physiological changes are manifested deeply in the increasing difficulty you have felt in praying for more than five minutes, spending time alone with your thoughts, and in deep reading of the Bible and other literature. I will also make the case that the attention economy is largely responsible for conditioning us to seek instant gratification, which leaves us constantly restless and unfulfilled. You will learn how "solitude deprivation," a new diagnosis for our era, is leaving us increasingly isolated, more informed yet less wise, more entertained yet less joyful.

The thesis of this book is that the abundant life is found in pursuing with all our being the disciplines found in the Bible such as solitude, prayer, and meditation. Through these disciplines we learn who we are in our Creator's eyes and, therefore, the meaning of our existence. It is only then that we are empowered to reject the trinkets of the culture's digital pleasures and confidently replace the time we previously used for the mindless pursuit of pleasure with tasks that create meaning in our life. This book is a journey. In any journey, we must have a clear understanding of both our destination and our starting point. To that end, I invite you to take a moment to honestly examine your starting point by taking the Smartphone Addiction Scale[2]. The Smartphone Addiction Scale (SAS)[1] is a widely used tool designed to assess the risk of smartphone addiction. It has been validated through several studies, showing good reliability and construct validity. The scale typically measures various dimensions such as daily-life disturbance,

---

2. https://www.healthyscreens.com/scale

positive anticipation, withdrawal, and tolerance, which are characteristic of behavioral addictions.

Now that you have a picture of your starting point on our journey, it is time to forget your past failures, press on to your destination, and reclaim your focus from the attention economy that seeks to fragment it. I will provide you with the tools to face this battle on two fronts: *individually*, by providing you with proven research on how to use three types of your attention on developing your passions as an antidote to distraction, and *systemically*, by helping you understand the world in which you live and the powerful design strategies of the attention economy that profit from your distraction. But more than anything else in this book, my deepest prayer is that you come to live the life Jesus calls you to—a life of deep connection, intentional solitude, and unwavering attention to the things that truly matter.

While I can't promise your life will be full as a result of reading this book, I can tell you that my life has been transformed through what I have learned. When I started studying this topic many years ago, I could feel the changes in my attention span and the incessant feeling of needing to check my device. My love of deep reading, prayer, and solitude were becoming increasingly difficult. Today, much has changed in my life as a result of what I am about to share with you. I have relearned to enjoy the transformative power of solitude. I have rekindled my love for reading Scripture and all kinds of books. Most importantly, I have deepened my relationship with my Creator and those around me through a mind that is able to focus again.

Just as you wouldn't embark on a journey without knowing where you're headed, you shouldn't live your life without clear focus and purpose. This book is your guide to reclaiming your attention and setting your course toward a life of deeper meaning, stronger faith, and true joy. Think of this book and your commitment to finish it as a manifesto for reclaiming your focus, your faith, and ultimately your life. In this age of distraction, commit now to put down your phone, look up, and join me on this journey. Together we will resist the pull of the digital world and embrace the peace, joy, and fulfillment that come from living in the presence of God.

Introduction

Do not conform to the pattern of this world,

but be transformed by the renewing of your mind.

–Romans 12:2

Aim at Heaven and you will get earth 'thrown in':

aim at earth and you will get neither.

–C.S. Lewis

"Grandpa, put down your phone! Look at this!"

Those words, spoken for the fourth time by my four-year-old grandson Flynn pierced through the digital fog enveloping my mind. To give my son and daughter-in-law a rare chance to spend some time away together, we had offered to watch our grandkids for the weekend. By the end of the weekend, after a full schedule of activities, I was exhausted. In a moment of fatigue, I sought refuge in my device, retreating from the real world into an endless stream of information and distractions.

"Huh?" I grunted, blinking as I surfaced from the depths of a never-ending scroll of news headlines, my mind far away from the room where I sat. Oblivious to the world around me, including the precious little boy standing a few feet away, I had missed the moment that truly mattered. After working on his Lego Star Wars Land Speeder for thirty minutes—an eternity for a four-year-old—Flynn was trying to unveil to me his finished product, a proud accomplishment in his young world. He was inviting me to share in his wonder and joy. But instead of celebrating with him, I looked up only to notice my grandson turning away with tears in his eyes, a dejected child who had given up after desperately trying to regain my focus. Flynn's plea was a wake-up call for me, a reminder of what truly matters and a commitment to regain control of my focus.

I'm sure you can relate to this scenario. We've all experienced the frustration and hurt of being ignored by someone engrossed in their phone, and we've all been guilty of doing the same to others. These moments of disconnection reveal a deeper issue in our lives: our struggle to maintain focus on what truly matters. Despite our best intentions, we often find ourselves drawn into the shallow allure of our devices, sacrificing meaningful interactions and experiences.

As an Information Systems professor at a Christian university, my dedication to studying technology and its impact on our lives is not merely theoretical. My own research on how to make technology more engaging, decades of experience working in the tech world, and personal interviews with industry insiders has allowed me to gain firsthand insights into the methods used to develop these technologies.

I have taught my students how to navigate this digital world responsibly and to cultivate a biblical worldview that prioritizes real-life connections over virtual ones. Yet despite all of this knowledge and experience, like the apostle Paul, I found myself in a battle between *knowledge* and *practice*. Paul's words in Romans 7:15–18 resonated deeply with me: "I do not understand what I do. For what I want to do I do not do, but what I hate I do. . . . For I do not do the good I want to do, but the evil I do not want to do—this I keep on doing." I knew the dangers of excessive screen time, but I struggled to apply that knowledge in my own life.

Join me on this journey: a journey to reclaim our focus from the attention economy that seeks to fragment it. It's a journey to reconnect with the abundant life Jesus promised, a life found not in the fleeting satisfaction of our devices but in the deep, lasting joy of spiritual practices like prayer, solitude, and reading the Bible. Since any battle must be won by offense and defense, this book is divided into three parts:

1. Offense: Learn what the attention economy is and how to diminish your need for distraction.

2. Defense: How to deepen your prayer, solitude, and deep reading in the attention economy.

3. Disconnecting from tech and reconnecting to the abundant life.

Part One—*Offense: The Attention Economy and The Antidote to Distraction*

In part one of the of the book we will first examine the systemic aspects of our technologies by looking at the attention economy and how it is contributing to your inability to focus. Specifically, we will see how millions of dollars and some of the brightest minds in the world are dedicated to capturing and maintaining your attention on your device. For example, we will see how specific design strategies used by big tech companies like the infinite scroll and algorithms can be used to capture and then maintain your attention. We will also learn to recognize the anatomy of our addictions and avoid the pull of getting our next "dopamine cookie" and avoid stress-inducing "cortisol loops." Finally, we will see how the designs of these tools shape us toward values that are sometimes contrary to the fruit of the Spirit, which we want to see in our lives.

Second, in part one, we will reconnect with the abundant life as the untapped antidote to distraction: developing a life full of gifts, abilities, and activities that demand our full attention. In the Gospel of John, Jesus says, "I have come that they may have life, and have it to the full" (John 10:10). This promise of abundant life is not about the quantity of our experiences but the quality of our connection with Him. It's about finding joy and contentment in His presence, even as the world clamors for our attention. Though much has been written on the power of a digital detox, we will learn from both the research and our own personal experiences that, by itself, this method generally falls short of our goals to engage deeply with our world and those around us. If you have ever experienced a digital detox, you know the pain, boredom, and mindlessness that is created when we choose to disconnect from our devices without something else to fill the vacuum of time we had previously allocated to our devices.

The critically unique point of this book is that before starting any digital detox, we must first define and identify the abundant life—a life filled in pursuit of our unique giftings that require our complete attention. To do this, we will learn how to counter the pull of our devices through a powerful theory in the research called "flow." Although the theory might sound like an eastern meditation practice, we will see that flow is something you have already experienced many times. We will start by learning how this type of extreme focus becomes an antidote to distraction. We will see how gamers, artists, and rock climbers all engage in activities that fill their life with complete focus and, critically, how this state of mind virtually eliminates the distractions of the attention economy. Using a powerful seven-step method starting with prayer, we will, like the man in Jesus' parable of the pearl of great price, happily give away our distractions for the things we truly value.

THE FOCUSED FAITH 11

Part Two—Defense: Elevating Solitude, Prayer, and Deep Reading in the Attention Economy

In part two, we will focus on the defensive front by learning how to view our technology biblically and how technology, if left unexamined, will fracture our ability to focus on the disciplines of our faith—solitude, prayer/meditation, and deep reading. We will start by defining technology biblically and then examine the importance of understanding the myth that our technologies are neutral, neither good nor bad. We will learn that the fight for our focus must be won by understanding the battle on two fronts—the individual and systemic. Individually, it is indeed my responsibility to put down my phone when I am around my grandson and those I love. However, we will also learn that there is a systemic element to overcoming our addiction. Every tool, including our digital ones, influences how we perceive reality. In other words, we will learn that while we influence our tools, they in turn influence us in sometimes unhealthy and unexpected ways. The key to freedom is in recognizing the values inherent in the technologies and how these values gently nudge us closer toward or away from our own values.

Next, in part two, we will look at three significant ways our tech, if left unexamined, is fracturing our Christian practices of solitude, prayer, and reading.

Solitude: We are the first generation in history that is never truly alone. For even when we are alone, our devices constantly demand our attention. Researchers have identified this phenomenon as "solitude deprivation." To counter solitude deprivation, we will, first, learn from Jesus', Elijah's, and King David's examples as well as how the great political and business leaders in our country, including Thomas Jefferson, Bill Gates, and Steve Wozniak, have all stated the critical importance of solitude. Second, we will learn the specific ways the attention economy is designed to work against our desire for solitude and practical steps we can take to "tame our tech." Finally, we will learn practical methods to carve out time for solitude in our lives by using the life changing one-hour daily digital fast and the transformative quarterly solitude retreat.

Prayer: We will explore the transformative research linking our attention to our prayer life. This chapter is informed by my advanced studies and personal interviews with spiritual leaders who have devoted their lives to the practice of prayer. We will learn that despite the endless distractions, developing three types of attention in our lives is possible: focused attention, rote attention, and boredom. Yes, boredom. We will develop our focused attention through practical methods such as the prayer walk and learning to "take captive every thought." Finally, we will learn how to hear the still, small voice of God as we develop our brains with the value of rote attention tasks like taking a shower, doing the dishes, and gardening.

Deep reading: I commend you for taking the time for reading this book. In this chapter, we will see how the superficial, fast-paced nature of the digital world is physiologically rewiring our brains and making it more difficult to read deeply. We will learn that, in addition to more shallow reading, we are reading less. Combined, we will see the fascinating research on how this lack of reading is impacting our ability to empathize with others. Finally, we will look at practical ways we can recapture our love for deep reading and to cultivate a life centered on the eternal truths of Scripture.

Part Three—*Disconnecting from Tech*

In part three, we will learn how to complete a digital detox while we aggressively pursue our uniquely gifted passions. We will learn the three critical lessons to perform after the detox by looking at the Amish's deliberate approach to selecting technologies that align with their values and rejecting those that negatively impact their faith or way of life. We will also see how adding "friction" is a powerful method shown to disrupt the automatic nature of device usage and encourage more mindful engagement with our technologies.

So let's begin. Join me in putting down your phone. Let us look up and see our husbands, wives, kids, grandkids, and our brothers and sisters in Christ anew. Join me in reconnecting with the beauty of the life God has given us. It's been too long. Together, we'll learn how to resist the pull of the digital world and embrace the peace and fulfillment that come from living in the presence of God. Let's reclaim our focus and live the abundant life Jesus calls us to. Let's embrace the joy of missing out on the superficial and dive deep into the richness of His love. Welcome to the journey of reclaiming our focus and discovering the abundant life in Christ!

Questions for Reflection

1. Read Romans 12:2. How does this verse challenge you to resist the influence of the attention economy? What practical steps can you take to "renew your mind" in today's digital age?

2. How has the attention economy affected your ability to engage in deep spiritual practices like prayer or Bible study?

3. Discuss the ways in which your digital habits either help or hinder your walk with God. What changes could you make to align more closely with your spiritual goals?

Lost in Scroll: Why Focus Feels Impossible

Be very careful, then, how you live—not as unwise but as wise, making the most of every opportunity, because the days are evil.

–Ephesians 5:15–16

For many of us, the great danger is not that we will renounce our faith, it is that we will become so distracted and rushed and preoccupied that we will settle for a mediocre version of it.

–John Ortberg

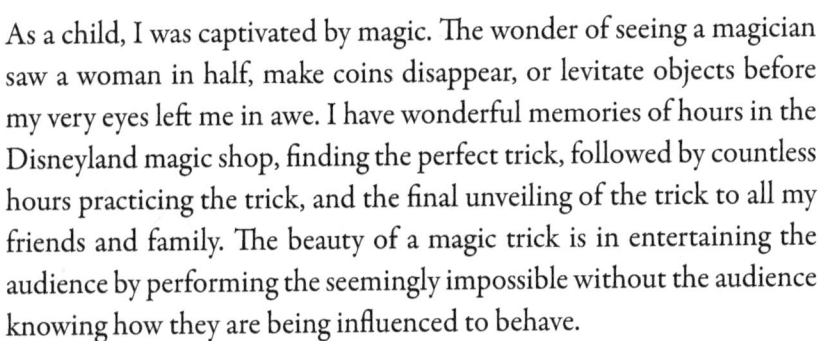

As a child, I was captivated by magic. The wonder of seeing a magician saw a woman in half, make coins disappear, or levitate objects before my very eyes left me in awe. I have wonderful memories of hours in the Disneyland magic shop, finding the perfect trick, followed by countless hours practicing the trick, and the final unveiling of the trick to all my friends and family. The beauty of a magic trick is in entertaining the audience by performing the seemingly impossible without the audience knowing how they are being influenced to behave.

One of my favorite tricks involved manipulating the audience's choices without their knowledge, and it never failed to leave the audience completely astounded. Here's how it worked: A person in the audience selected a card and inserted it back into the deck without my knowing the selected card. Using some sleight of hand, I moved that card to the top of the deck and then shuffled the cards, while being careful to keep the selected card on top. I then laid out the cards, face down, into four piles without the audience knowing that I knew the exact location of the selected card and pile. My favorite part of the trick was what happened next—the point that the audience's choices were seriously manipulated without their knowing. I instructed the audience to "pick two piles." If the audience picked one of the piles that had their selected card, I would remove the other two piles. Conversely, if the audience picked the piles that did not have the selected card, I would remove those two piles. So no matter what piles the audience selected, I either removed or kept them to make sure the audience's card would always remain. The key to this trick is that I was intentionally vague in saying, "Pick two piles," instead of something like, "Pick two piles to remove." I then continued this process until there was only one card remaining, which left the audience completely dumbfounded how they magically selected their own card from all the cards in the deck!

In my years spent researching the attention economy, I've found myself reflecting on this childhood love of magic when considering the complexities of our modern digital world. Today, tech companies have become the new magicians employing their own brand of "magic" to captivate our attention. But unlike the innocent wonder of childhood magic, the tricks used by these digital illusionists are designed to manipulate and exploit our cognitive processes. Their goal is not to amaze or entertain but to capture and hold our focus for profit—often without our even realizing the extent of their influence.

In the same way that I manipulated the audience to select their own card, I have learned that tech companies use sophisticated algorithms and psychological insights to manipulate us in order to keep us engaged with their platforms. Notifications, infinite scrolling, and personalized content streams are the digital equivalents of a magician's flourish, drawing us deeper into their world and away from the real one. This modern magic preys on our natural tendencies and desires, turning our attention into a commodity that can be bought, sold, and manipulated for profit.

While my childhood experiences with magic were harmless and filled with joy, the magic of tech companies operates in a more insidious manner. It subtly alters our behaviors, reshapes our interactions, and diminishes our capacity for deep and meaningful engagement with others and our faith.

Reasons for Studying the Attention Economy

I believe there are at least three reasons for you to join me in my journey to understand why it is important to understand the attention economy. First, we need to understand that a significant reason for our lack of focus is not our fault. The path to renewed focus certainly involves making personal changes to our lives, but there are systemic issues that we must understand in order to better identify and successfully make these changes. Second, understanding this problem helps us understand the impact the attention economy is making on our world. Retaining and focusing our attention is arguably the most valuable endeavor for the brilliant minds in our world to continue to be able to live out lives in the image of our God in creating new products and services. Finally, as we clearly understand the attention economy, we can work together to find solutions, both within the church and for society as a whole.

Introduction: Defining the Attention Economy

The term "attention economy" was first coined by Michael H. Goldhaber in his 1997 article, "The Attention Economy and the Net," published in the journal *First Monday*.[2] Goldhaber explored how the internet and digital technologies were shifting the economic landscape from one focused on material goods to one centered around capturing and monetizing human attention. His article laid the groundwork for understanding how attention became a scarce and valuable commodity in the digital age.

More recently, the term "attention capitalism" builds on the concept of the attention economy referring to the economic system in which human attention is treated as a scarce commodity and monetized by businesses, primarily through advertising. This model is prevalent in the digital age, where platforms like Google, Facebook, and X generate revenue by capturing and retaining user attention. *The goal is to maximize the amount of time users spend on their platforms, which in turn increases the value of the advertising space.* According to Tim Wu, the scholar who coined the term attention capitalism, these companies leverage advanced technology and psychological insights to keep users engaged, often at the cost of their mental health and well-being.[3] This model has profound implications for individuals and society, including Christians, who are called to live mindful and intentional lives.

Big Tech and the Motivation to Capture Attention

As of this writing, the combined revenue for Google in the last five years is 1.192 *trillion* dollars.[4] Have you ever considered why companies like Google, and others in the attention economy like Facebook, and X, are so successful without ever asking for a penny from you? The way these companies have been so successful is by applying some sleight of hand to capture your attention without your knowing it and then selling it to the businesses who pay to deliver targeted advertising to you based on what Google knows about you. Tristan Harris, a former developer for Google and now founder of the Ethical Center for Humanity, has summarized this well, saying, "If you're not paying for the product, you are the product."[5]

To illustrate how this works, consider an example we are all familiar with: researching and purchasing a product online. In this case, consider the experience of my wife and I when we needed to replace our couch and loveseat. We began our search using Google with search terms like "furniture stores near me." We shopped online, looking at the inventory of couches in nearby stores. We also used Facebook Marketplace to look into gently used options. Within one day, my wife noticed that the abundance of ads in her social media accounts were dedicated to sofas and loveseats. Another common example is how we may comment, "I swear my phone hears my conversations," as the ads delivered to us are seemingly magically targeted to our interests—even in cases where we believe we haven't supplied the information online.

So, what sort of sleight of hand are the digital magicians employing to do this trick? This seamless targeting happens because companies like Google and Facebook track our online activities, gathering data on our interests, preferences, and behaviors. Every search query, website visit, and social media interaction is logged and analyzed to build a comprehensive profile of each user. This data is then used to deliver personalized advertisements, ensuring that the ads we see are relevant to our current needs and interests. For businesses, like those selling couches in my example, this targeted advertising is incredibly valuable as it allows them to reach potential customers who are most likely to be interested in their products. The success of this model is reflected in Google's massive revenue, demonstrating the power and profitability of the attention economy.

Effects of Attention Economy

At first glance, we might conclude there really isn't a problem with this business model. After all, what is the problem with Google understanding my digital profile and helping me in my search for a couch or other products it knows about me? The problem is that the attention economy relies solely on your engagement. In order to build your digital profile, these companies employ some of the brightest minds in the world to capture and keep your attention, and this results in endless distractions from the people and things you value most in life. The more time you spend on these platforms, the more data they generate, which in turn can be monetized through targeted advertising. The research is clear that the end result of the attention economy is addiction and the inability to focus, along with stress, anger, and intolerance.

Internet Addiction

The most vulnerable to the effects of the addictive nature of the attention economy are our young people. Recent research has shown several troubling conclusions. One comprehensive study tracked the smartphone use of 203 teenagers, revealing a median smartphone use of more than four hours per day, with some teens using their phones for more than sixteen hours a day.[6] These devices were picked up and checked a median of fifty-one times per day, with the highest number of pickups reaching 498 in a single day. This frequent engagement with smartphones is driven by numerous notifications—half of the participants received 237 or more notifications daily, leading to constant distractions and interruptions.

The content consumption patterns highlight the captivating power of certain apps. For instance, TikTok was used by 50 percent of the participants for a median of nearly two hours per day, with some users spending upwards of seven hours daily on the platform. The app's design, which involves automatic video playback and highly personalized content recommendations, ensures minimal user effort and maximum engagement. This irresistible draw is further amplified by the algorithm's ability to quickly adapt to user preferences, making the app even more addictive.

In a broader context, digital consumption has dramatically increased over the years. A significant percentage of teens are heavily reliant on their devices, with 85 percent of teens aged thirteen to seventeen using YouTube, 72 percent using Instagram, and 69 percent using

Snapchat.[7] Gloria Mark, one of the leading researchers in attention, reminds us these types of statistics are especially troubling for youth because their self-control and executive functions are not yet mature. These functions develop throughout childhood, reaching similar competencies to adults at around age ten.[8] In a study that examined twenty-two students participating in a twenty-four hour fast from their phones, students used terms like "unbearable," "miserable," "jittery," "very anxious," and "in withdrawal" to describe the experience.[9]

Lest we think the problem is limited to our youth, the reality is we have all become addicted to our smartphones. One study showed that the compulsion to engage in social media can be more difficult to resist than the desire for tobacco, coffee, alcohol, and eating.[10] Another study showed the average person checks their cellphone 144 times per day![11] This equates to once every ten minutes! This relentless drive for engagement has resulted in a staggering 40 percent of the population exhibiting some form of internet-based addiction, with many individuals unable to imagine life without their smartphones. Most of these are not conscious choices. Rather, the companies creating the platforms on our devices are getting better at keeping us addicted through a chemical called "dopamine."

Anatomy of Addiction: Dopamine and Cortisol

While there are many facets to being addicted to our devices, two chemicals play a huge role through physiological impacting our body: dopamine and cortisol. Dopamine has been termed the "molecule of more" because the more we trigger the release of dopamine, the more we will want our next "shot." Meurisse reminds us that, contrary to popular belief, dopamine is not itself a pleasure chemical.[12] Dopamine is a neurotransmitter that makes us *anticipate* pleasure. It is the same chemical that is generated when we anticipate eating or addictive drugs. The reality, however, is that the generation of the chemical does not mean you actually receive the expected pleasure. Generally, the experience is the opposite with technologies such as social media notifications. When you see a notification, you anticipate a reward you will receive, such as seeing likes or comments to your posts, which triggers dopamine in your brain. When you check your stats on your financial portfolio or your performance at work, you expect a reward from seeing positive numbers. When you visit YouTube, you expect to see interesting or engaging videos. All of these expectations trigger the release of dopamine. The reality is that we are generally left feeling empty and unfulfilled.

We can see a good example of how this cycle works when looking at how dopamine functions for drug and alcohol addicts. Addiction generates a continuous triggering of the release of dopamine, which ultimately strengthens tolerance to this stimulation. As a result, the drug addict needs progressively stronger doses to experience the same sense of pleasure. Even after the addict realizes the drug has ruined his life, the brain continues to stimulate dopamine because it remembers it soothed a need in the past. In the same way, as we begin to realize the shallow and negative aspects of technologies in our life, we continue to want more—just as we did when they still made us happy.

The other chemical, cortisol, is a hormone released by the adrenal glands in response to stress. It is part of the body's fight-or-flight response mechanism and plays a crucial role in regulating various bodily functions, including metabolism, immune response, and stress response. In the context of our technology, researchers[13] have studied cortisol loops. The cortisol loop refers to the cycle of stress and behavior that can be perpetuated by the frequent checking of our smartphones. Here is how it works:

Triggering Event: When you receive a notification or hear a phone alert, the body responds by releasing cortisol.

Stress Response: The release of cortisol triggers a stress response, leading to heightened alertness and a sense of urgency.

Behavioral Reaction: To alleviate this stress, you check your phone, seeking relief by addressing the notification.

Temporary Relief: While checking the phone might provide temporary relief, it often introduces new information or stimuli that can trigger further stress.

Cycle Continuation: This leads to a repetitive cycle where you continually check your phone, leading to a perpetual loop of cortisol release and stress. Neuroendocrinologists have highlighted how even just the sight or sound of a phone can trigger cortisol release, even if the notification is not immediately checked. This creates a loop where the stress of potential notifications drives the need to check the phone, which in turn leads to more stress.

Fragmented Attention

The attention economy is having broad effects on our ability to focus. Studies show that the average duration of attention on a screen before switching to another screen is declining. Gloria Mark's research reveals that our attention spans while using digital devices have become extremely short, averaging about forty-seven seconds on any given screen.[14] This decline in attention span is not just limited to work environments but extends to personal and social contexts as well. The frequent switching of tasks and interruptions caused by notifications can lead to cognitive overload and stress. Mark's research has shown that multitasking and continuous partial attention result in decreased performance, increased errors, and higher stress levels.[15]

In researching this book, I interviewed Samuel James, author of *Digital Liturgies* and a number of other excellent books. James pointed out that the fragmentation of attention is not just a personal issue but also a cultural one. There is something about working on a screen that makes it more difficult to focus. And especially with the advance of artificial intelligence taking on increasing roles, there needs to be a cultural shift in defining "fulfilling" work, a shift towards a reevaluation of what the abundant life looks like in our vocations. James explained it to me like this:

> If you're a construction worker or contractor or something like that, then your default might be different than an information worker. So, an information worker might actually have to think more holistically about how to reenter their attention. . . . There is something about physical work and the tactile experience that actually enables and empowers being in the moment more than information work.

In general, I think we all sense this feeling of losing control of our attention. How many times have we regretted tuning out with our phone while our child pleads for our attention? Or how often do we regret simply enjoying a moment without the urge to take the picture so we can share it with others? Tristan Harris, in a *60 Minutes* interview, explained that our lack of control is not entirely due to a lack of self-discipline.[16] It is, instead, because billions of dollars have been invested to make this outcome inevitable. In the interview Harris said, "There's always this narrative that technology's neutral. And it's up to us to choose how we use it. This is just not true. . . . It's not neutral. They want you to use it in particular ways and for long periods of time. Because that's how they make their money." Harris is now a leader in providing growing awareness that the attention economy drives companies like Google into a "race to the bottom of the brain stem."[17] The key to improving our lives and our focus, therefore, is to better understand the tactics used by these companies.

Anger and Intolerance

Aside from internet addiction and lack of focus, the research is increasingly clear that culturally we are becoming more angry and less tolerant of other viewpoints. For example, Jonathon Hari discusses research in his book on how the way to get the most views on YouTube is to include words like "hates," "obliterates," "slams," or "destroys" in your title.[18] Words that will increase your retweet rate are "attack," "bad," and "blame." There is a popular saying on the internet that sums up the research well: "If it's more enraging, it's more engaging."

Besides fostering anger in ourselves, and ultimately in society, social media platforms contribute to the creation of knowledge silos or "echo chambers" that can foster intolerance.[19] These sites are driven by algorithms which are designed to maximize user engagement by curating content that aligns our individual preferences and beliefs. Consequently, we are exposed primarily to information that reinforces our existing viewpoints, creating these echo chambers where dissenting perspectives are rarely encountered.

Designed for Addiction

The addictive nature of the attention economy is intricately tied to the design strategies employed by technology companies to capture and sustain our focus. In 2009, Stanford researcher B. J. Fogg introduced "behavior design," a discipline rooted in the principles of behaviorism.[20] This approach posits that behavior change occurs when three elements converge: motivation (wanting to do it), ability (being able to do it), and prompts (being triggered to do it). Fogg's behavior design draws from classic behaviorist principles, much like B. F. Skinner's work with operant conditioning and reinforcement, which demonstrated how behaviors could be shaped through rewards and punishments.

Fogg's behavior design framework has been used to create highly engaging digital experiences by leveraging intermittent rewards and other persuasive techniques to capture and retain users' attention. This methodology has raised ethical questions about the responsibility of tech designers in creating products that can lead to addictive behaviors and diminish users' control over their attention and time.

Harris and many other tech leaders today studied under Fogg at Stanford and learned how to apply these principles to the design of digital products. Harris, who was previously a Google project manager, has since become vocal about the ethical concerns surrounding these techniques, particularly in how they exploit users' psychological vulnerabilities to increase engagement. He likens the repetitive checking of apps and notifications to Skinner's rats, which were conditioned to press levers in the hope of receiving unpredictable rewards.[21]

There are at least four key design strategies used by the big tech companies to keep us engaged: the like button, the infinite scroll, notifications, and algorithms.

Like button: The very essence of the like button, established by Facebook in 2009, has redefined online social interaction by creating a simple-yet-powerful tool that allows people to show their appreciation or support for literally any piece of content. The problem with the like button is that studies have found that chasing likes stimulates the reward centers of the brain, most notably through the release of dopamine, with mechanisms very much akin to those seen in gambling. This can cause compulsive behaviors where we continuously attempt to seek and feel validated by likes and get into a feedback loop that strengthens social comparisons and in some instances leads to anxiety and depression, especially among the teen and young adult populations.[22] The reward centers in the brains of adolescents are especially sensitive; this means that the amount of dopamine activated in response to likes associates with greater sensitivity to social rewards and reinforcement with use.[23] The continual quest for approval leads to checking social media profiles again and again, thus reducing attention span and at the same time heightening feelings of inadequacy.[24] The good news is that research has also shown that decreasing the use of social media—and, therefore, exposure to these cycles of validation—can help decrease feelings of loneliness and depression.[25]

Infinite scroll: Aza Raskin, now co-founder of "Center for Humane Technology," was a designer and technologist and inventor the concept of infinite scroll, a feature now ubiquitous across social media platforms and various websites. Infinite scroll allows users to continue consuming content without the need to click to the next page, creating a seamless and uninterrupted flow of information. While the design was initially intended to enhance user experience by making content more accessible, Raskin has since expressed concerns about its impact on our lives. In Hari's book *Stolen Focus*, Raskin discusses how he has calculated that infinite scroll increases time spent on sites like X by approximately 50 percent, which on a global scale, amounts to the equivalent of 200,000 human lifetimes being consumed by scrolling rather than engaging in other activities.[26]

Notifications: Notifications are designed to create a sense of urgency and continuous engagement. Big tech companies rely on these design elements as comparable to the intermittent reinforcement used in gambling, as highlighted by B. F. Skinner's behavioral psychology principles, where unpredictable rewards encourage repeated behavior.[27] These notifications serve as constant prompts to return to our devices, creating a cycle of frequent engagement and distraction. This pattern is exacerbated by the fact that apps like Snapchat and Discord send numerous notifications, encouraging users to continually check their phones throughout the day.

Algorithms: Algorithms play a critical role in sustaining attention by learning and adapting to user preferences. For example, TikTok's algorithm quickly adapts to a user's interests, ensuring that the content served is highly engaging and relevant.[28] This low-friction interaction, where videos start playing automatically without requiring any user action, makes it easy for users to spend hours on the platform without even realizing it. The types of algorithms vary, but they all have one thing in common: They will show you things to ensure that you keep your eyes on the screen.

Confessions of Big Tech

One possible reaction to this research is that the tech companies are not knowingly trying to generate addiction to our devices. Indeed, the people behind these companies are some of the brightest people in the world. And they certainly seem ethical. That said, when we look closely at these companies, the overriding business model of capturing our attention at all costs has been the *stated focus since the beginning.*

As evidence, consider the following powerful quote from Sean Parker, founder of Napster and first president of Facebook, regarding the thought process in building these applications:

> How do we consume as much of your time and conscious attention as possible? . . . We need to sort of give you a little dopamine hit every once in a while, because someone

THE FOCUSED FAITH

liked or commented on a photo or a post or whatever. And that's going to get you to contribute more content, and that's going to get you . . . more likes and comments. . . . It's a social-validation feedback loop . . . exactly the kind of thing that a hacker like myself would come up with, because you're exploiting a vulnerability in human psychology. . . . The inventors, creators—it's me, it's Mark [Zuckerberg], it's Kevin Systrom on Instagram, it's all of these people—understood this consciously. . . . And we did it anyway.[29]

Similarly, Chamath Palihapitiya, the former Vice President for User Growth at Facebook, has been a vocal critic of the very platform he helped to grow. In various public statements, Palihapitiya has expressed "tremendous guilt" for the role he played in creating tools that he believes are "ripping apart the social fabric of how society works."[30] He has highlighted the manipulative power built into social media systems, particularly emphasizing the "short-term, dopamine-driven feedback loops" that social media platforms use to keep users engaged. These loops, driven by features such as likes and comments, are designed to exploit psychological vulnerabilities, resulting in increased engagement but also fostering misinformation, lack of civil discourse, and societal division. Palihapitiya has also pointed out the broader implications of these practices, including their global impact. He mentioned specific incidents, such as the spread of hoaxes via WhatsApp leading to violent outcomes, to illustrate how these platforms can be manipulated by bad actors to achieve harmful ends. His candid admissions have contributed to a growing awareness of the ethical and societal implications of social media and the need for more responsible design and regulation of these technologies.[31] Other Facebook developers, Justin Rosenstein and Leah Pearlman, who were part of the team that developed the like button, later expressed regret over its far-reaching negative impacts. They noted that the button encourages users to seek validation and popularity, which can lead to addiction and emotional distress.

Steve Jobs, the co-founder of Apple, limited his children's use of technology, including the iPad, despite it's being one of his company's flagship products.[32] He believed in the importance of limiting screen time to foster healthier habits and real-world interactions. Similarly, Bill Gates, the founder of Microsoft, did not allow his children to have cell phones until they were fourteen years old and imposed strict limits on their screen time. Gates emphasized the need for balance, and ensured that devices were not used during family meals in order to encourage more personal interactions. Finally, Chris Anderson, the former editor of *Wired* magazine and CEO of 3D Robotics, also set stringent tech usage rules for his children, acknowledging the addictive nature of these technologies. He mentioned that having witnessed the dangers of technology firsthand, he wanted to prevent his kids from falling into the same traps.[33]

Attention Economy for Christians

For Christians, the attention economy poses significant challenges to living out our faith. Jay Kim's book *Analog Christian* is helpful in contrasting how the attention economy is often at odds with fruit of the spirit. In Galatians 5:22–25 Paul writes, "But the fruit of the Spirit is love, joy, peace, forbearance, kindness, goodness, faithfulness, gentleness, and self-control. Against such things there is no law. Those who belong to Christ Jesus have crucified the flesh with its passions and desires. Since we live by the Spirit, let us keep in step with the Spirit."

The last verse is critical. In order to live by the Spirit, we must keep in step with the Spirit. Kim points out that keeping in step with the Spirit requires us to daily choose the fruits of the Spirit rather than what the

THE FOCUSED FAITH

attention economy has to offer. Specifically, we can choose to cultivate fruit in multiple areas that the attention economy is designed to work against.

Self-Control over Reckless Indulgence

As we have seen, the attention economy has been designed to make us creatures of reckless indulgence, ever seeking the next hit of dopamine. Tim Keller said, "Self-control is the ability to do the important thing rather than the urgent thing."[34] As Christians, we must ask the Spirit of God to help us develop the gift of self-control and undo the urgent and endless pull of our digital world. The Proverbs are full of reminders to develop self-control and develop hearts that are focused on doing the important things in life rather than the urgent things.

Patience over Impatience

We will learn more in future chapters how the internet and the technologies of our day have impacted our ability for patience in areas such as reading. Many of us struggle to sit in quiet meditation without feeling the need to fill the silence in our minds with digital dopamine cookies. Biblically, we must learn to fight against this urge and wait on Him. "The Lord is good to those whose hope is in him, to the one who seeks him; it is good to wait quietly for the salvation of the Lord" (Lamentations 3:25–26). Kim reminds us what we all intuitively know within our heart:

> The stuff of life that truly matters is never that accessible. And yet, paradoxically, it's much more accessible than we can imagine. But it's found not in the easy and convenient comforts of online life. The things that truly matter—life-giving relationships, the sacrifices that infuse life with meaning, destiny-defining struggles and triumphs—these things and more require patience. They

require a willingness to enter into pain and find on the other side a life truly worth living.[35]

Joy over Comparison

We have all heard or experienced the term FOMO: Fear of Missing Out. It refers to the anxiety or fear that we feel, especially with social media, when we are missing out on social events, experiences, or interactions that others are enjoying. The attention economy perpetuates the problem as research has shown that social media significantly increases depression and loneliness; especially for young girls and women.[36] Our perception of our own appearance decreases as we see the curated images of others who seem to have a much better body, life, job, or you fill in the blank. Kim writes, "Genuine joy is not in someplace or in becoming someone. Rather, joy is found and made complete as we remain in Jesus, the vine, and the giver of true joy."[37]

In response to FOMO, I propose that we work to develop JOMO, a term growing in popularity that stands for Joy of Missing Out. JOMO embraces the satisfaction and contentment that comes from choosing to step away from the hectic pace of the attention economy and the constant connectivity that technology often imposes. In contrast to constant comparison, we can instead choose to disconnect from addictive behaviors, embrace solitude, read, pray, and fully pursue the abundant life that God has promised us instead.

The attention economy has fragmented our ability to focus, and it feels as if we are constantly scrolling without end. But there is hope: the antidote to this distracted mind lies in something far deeper: flow states that allow us to fully engage with the present moment. In the next chapter, we will explore how finding flow can reconnect us to the abundant life God has promised.

Application Guide

For a detailed checklist to evaluate and reduce your digital habits, download the Application Guide by visiting here[1]. You'll find practical steps to begin reclaiming your focus today.

Key Points

❖ The attention economy employs its own magic tricks to captivate and manipulate our focus.

❖ Take the first step toward regaining control over your attention by understanding these digital manipulations.

❖ Evaluate your digital habits and begin the process of reducing the influence of these manipulations on your daily life.

Questions for Reflection

1. Read Ephesians 5:15-16. How does this passage relate to your use of digital devices? What changes can you make to "make the most of every opportunity" in your daily life?

2. Have you noticed a decline in your ability to focus? What practices or habits have contributed to this, and how might you reverse the trend?

3. Consider the concept of "fragmented focus." How can understanding this concept help you reclaim your attention?

---

1. https://www.thefocusedfaith.com/free

Flowing into Abundance: The True Cure for a Distracted Mind

The kingdom of heaven is like treasure hidden in a field.

When a man found it, he hid it again,

and then in his joy went and sold all he had and bought that field.

–Matthew 13:44

The settled happiness and security which we all desire,

God withholds from us by the very nature of the world:

but joy, pleasure, and merriment, He has scattered broadcast.

–C.S. Lewis

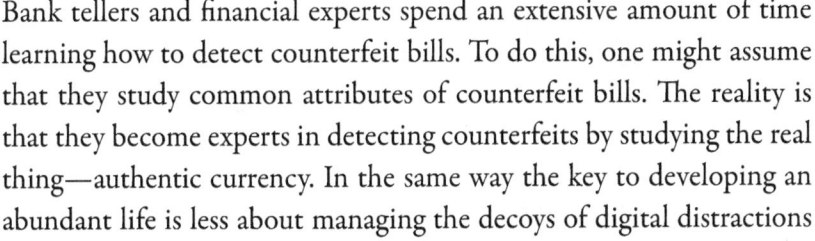

Bank tellers and financial experts spend an extensive amount of time learning how to detect counterfeit bills. To do this, one might assume that they study common attributes of counterfeit bills. The reality is that they become experts in detecting counterfeits by studying the real thing—authentic currency. In the same way the key to developing an abundant life is less about managing the decoys of digital distractions that surround us and more about learning how to detect and pursue the real thing—abundant life.

C. S. Lewis offers the closest example of a biblical description of the abundant life:

> Give up yourself, and you will find your real self. Lose your life and you will save it. Submit to death, death of your

> ambitions and favorite wishes every day and death of your whole body in the end: submit with every fiber of your being, and you will find eternal life. Keep back nothing. Nothing that you have not given away will be really yours. Nothing in you that has not died will ever be raised from the dead. Look for yourself, and you will find in the long run only hatred, loneliness, despair, rage, ruin, and decay. But look for Christ and you will find Him, and with Him everything else thrown in.[38]

In reading these powerful words, I am both inspired and convicted. I am inspired to find my true joy and abundant life as a husband, father, and academic. Yet the words remind me of the many times that I drift back to seeking worldly pleasures instead of the abundant life promised in Christ. I think the vast majority of us living in today's digital world have felt this too. Mark Fisher, a British cultural critic and humanist, put a name to this feeling: depressive hedonia. In his book, *Capitalist Realism: Is There No Alternative?* he explains that the feeling that something is missing is derived from our culture's inability to do anything except pursue pleasure.[39] The culture, according to Fisher, is rooted in a relentless pursuit of pleasure and instant gratification, and this pursuit ultimately leads to a feeling of emptiness and dissatisfaction.

The digital world and the attention economy provide a temporary but constant flow of "pleasure" for us to pursue. The irony is that this pursuit leads us to be continually distracted and ultimately unfulfilled. In *The Shallows* Nicholas Carr writes how the internet has turned us into "lab rats constantly pressing levers to get tiny pellets of social or intellectual nourishment."[40] Any "pleasure" we desire is but a scroll, click or swipe away.

The reality is that the abundant life is not found in the scroll, click, or swipe. It is also not found by going through digital detox. When we try to unplug from social media for a day or week, we are often left with a void of empty time that we previously filled with our devices. The result is we feel cut off from the people and friendships around us. The research seems to support the futility of hoping a digital detox alone will solve our problems. Cal Newport is a bestselling author on the topic and summarizes his research this way: "I've become convinced that what you need instead is a full-fledged philosophy of technology use, rooted in your deep values, that provides clear answers to the questions of what tools you should use and how you should use them and, equally important, enables you to confidently ignore everything else."[41]

I couldn't agree more. We need a philosophy of technology use rooted in our deep values. For the Christian, our deep values are derived from the Word of God. The thesis of this book, therefore, is that the abundant life is found in pursuing with all our being the disciplines found in the Bible such as solitude, prayer, and meditation. Through these disciplines we learn who we are in our Creator's eyes and, therefore, the meaning of our existence. It is only then that we are empowered to reject the trinkets of the culture's digital pleasures and confidently replace the time we previously used for the mindless pursuit of pleasure with tasks that create meaning in our life.

Reconnect with Your Gifts and Passions

In the parable of the pearl of great price, Jesus said, "The kingdom of heaven is like treasure hidden in a field. When a man found it, he hid it again, and then in his joy went and sold all he had and bought that field. Again, the kingdom of heaven is like a merchant looking for fine pearls. When he found one of great value, he went away and sold everything he had and bought it" (Matthew 13:44–46).

The key point in the parable is that the man in the parable happily gave away his possessions because they were a distraction from what he valued—the treasure. Mahatma Gandhi, in talking about a life of voluntary simplicity, is attributed as saying, "Only give up a thing when you want some other condition so much the thing no longer has any attraction for you, or when it seems to interfere with that which is more great desired."[42]

The first step to reject the pull of our tech and enter into the abundant life Jesus described is for us to identify and pursue His kingdom in a way that makes us willingly give up everything else. So how exactly do we develop this type of passion for His kingdom that leads us to willingly reject the modern distractions of our day? Stay with me, and we will explore some significant research that will help us develop powerful passions for the kingdom and experience the abundant life. But before we get to that, let me share an unlikely topic of my study in grad school that ultimately led me to find a path to my passions: the study of gamers.

As a young child I was, like the vast majority youth, captured and addicted to video games. I am dating myself here, but I have wonderful memories of playing games on Atari and later Commodore 64. I spent countless hours, along with every other kid on the block, completely captured by games like PacMan, Donkey Kong, and Asteroids. Every day brought a new challenge for me to get to the next level of the game or see my name appear on a leaderboard. Like so many gamers today, four hours of gaming would feel like twenty minutes.

Fast forward to grad school, I was interested in researching ways technology could improve both academic and business goals. This led into research on developing "user engagement" in information systems and a concept called "gamification." Gamification is defined as the addition of game-like elements such as leaderboards, points, or levels to non-game applications.[43] The easiest example of gamification is a fitness app that tracks your progress toward your fitness goals and sometimes compares your performance with others.

The concept of gamification made perfect sense to me. I could instantly see the power of how adding gamification elements such as leaderboards or levels to non-game applications could generate more engagement with the information system. During graduate school, I was also working full time as a professor, teaching online courses in information systems that relied heavily on online discussions for students to engage with the course. In several of these courses, students reported to me that the online discussion board was unchallenging and, therefore, often ignored. In thinking of how to make the online discussion board more interesting, I wondered about the potential power of adding gamification elements, specifically leaderboards and digital badges. Without going into all of the details, the results were astonishing. I completed multiple studies and a dissertation showing that adding gamification elements to a leaderboard resulted in significant increases to both the quantity of posts and quality of the posts as reflected in overall grades in the course. Simply put, students were much more engaged in discussions that used gamification.

Flow Theory

There is a powerful concept that explains the reasons why my students, and anyone who has participated in a form of gamification, becomes more engaged with technology: flow theory. Flow theory, developed by psychologist Mihaly Csikszentmihalyi, describes a mental state of complete absorption in an activity, where a person loses track of time and is fully engaged in the task at hand.[44] Though the name might lead one to believe it is an Eastern meditation practice, it is not. It is an experience you are already familiar with and could be simply described as those times when you felt you are totally focused and "in the zone." Csikszentmihalyi identifies several key characteristics of flow:

1. **Intense Focus and Concentration:** During flow, individuals experience a heightened state of concentration, where distractions fade away, and attention is solely focused on the activity.

2. **Merging of Action and Awareness:** There is a seamless integration of action and awareness, where individuals feel at one with what they are doing.

3. **Loss of Self-consciousness:** Self-awareness diminishes, and individuals become less concerned with themselves and more with the activity.

4. **Sense of Control:** Participants feel a sense of mastery and control over the task, even if it is challenging.

5. **Intrinsic Reward:** The activity itself is rewarding, providing deep satisfaction and joy.

As I thought about this theory, I thought back to my childhood and the way time would fly by as I pursued the next level on the newest game. The research on flow theory shows that gamers enter a state of flow when they are deeply immersed in a game that provides the right balance of challenge and skill. Leaderboards, and other gamification elements such as digital badges or points, play a significant role in facilitating flow by providing clear goals and immediate feedback through three aspects that promote engagement:

1. **Clear Objectives:** Games with clear goals and objectives help players focus their efforts and understand what needs to be achieved.

2. **Immediate Feedback:** Leaderboards and in-game feedback systems offer real-time responses to players' actions, allowing them to adjust their strategies and stay engaged.

3. **Balanced Challenges:** Games that match the player's skill level with appropriate challenges help maintain flow. Too easy, and the game becomes boring; too hard, and it becomes frustrating.[45]

Are you still with me? If not, the research on this is clear: *Flow theory is not limited to games. It has powerful applications to many other life domains.*

Artists, musicians, and performers often describe flow as a state of effortless creativity, where they lose track of time and become one with their art. Athletes frequently report being in flow during competitions when they are fully immersed in the physical and mental demands of their sport. Professionals often enter a state of flow when they are engaged in tasks that are meaningful, challenging, and align with their skills. For instance, a software developer might experience flow while coding, or a writer while crafting a story.

Another powerful example in my life is fishing. Much of this book was written while on sabbatical in the Sierra Nevada mountains. When I wasn't writing the book, I would take a break and fish on the Hamilton Branch of Lake Almanor. The summer fishing here is some of the best in the world. As I wrote about flow states, I realized my time spent fishing was a powerful example of flow. While there were many people fishing on the creek, absolutely nobody was checking their phones. I believe this underscores the critical point of this book: *There is tremendous power in filling your life with flow states as an antidote to the mindless distractions we find on our phones.*

While fishing, I find it hard to even think about taking time to eat. Time is lost on everyone fishing along this stream; they're all fully focused on catching fish. What exactly is it that puts everyone fishing here on Lake Almanor into flow? I believe the answer is because it perfectly meets the three conditions of entering a flow state. First, there is a clear objective: catch fish. Second, there is immediate feedback. During this time of year, there are thousands of fish in this stream and my bobber consistently provides me with clear feedback no more than once every ten minutes letting me know the fish are interested in what's on my hook. Finally, the challenge is appropriate. If I were able to catch my limit easily within one hour, I may not be as focused. Conversely, if the fish were so big that I couldn't land them or so little that they weren't bigger than the bait, I would give up. The challenge/skill balance of the activity seems to be set perfectly to ensure that I dedicate my full attention to the task.

In all of these examples, we experience flow when we enter into a deep focus on the task at hand that we are passionate about—the exact opposite mental state of checking our phones for the latest notification or YouTube video. Flow stands in stark contrast to the distracted state perpetuated by the attention economy. While distractions fragment our attention and diminish our ability to focus, flow consolidates our mental resources, leading to deep engagement and fulfillment in at least three ways:

> 1. **Enhanced Focus:** Flow eliminates distractions by demanding full attention and engagement in the activity. In general, we are vulnerable to distractions whenever we work on a task that fails to interest us or hold our attention. Distractions can take two forms: internal and external. Internal distractions include things like lack of self-confidence or allowing our minds to wander. External distractions include everything outside of our minds, such

as our phones, people around us, and other external interruptions. Flow states provide the superpower ability to ignore the world around us and focus fully on the things that matter.

2. **Deep Satisfaction:** Unlike the fleeting gratification from social media or other distractions, flow provides intrinsic rewards that lead to lasting satisfaction. *The key element of a flow state is elevated contentment with our current situation.* Our devices attempt to offer us satisfaction but always leave us wanting more. A life filled with multiple flow states is one that aligns with our interests and, therefore, generates deep satisfaction.

3. **Productivity and Mastery:** Flow enhances productivity and fosters a sense of mastery, as we become fully engaged in improving our skills and achieving our goals.

From a Christian perspective, the concept of flow aligns beautifully with the idea of living an abundant life. Jesus said, "I have come that they may have life, and have it to the full" (John 10:10). Here is one of the most critical points of this book: *Just as flow requires intense focus on an activity, an abundant Christian life involves focusing our hearts and minds on God through tasks leading to the deep satisfaction that can only be found in communing with our Creator through tasks such as prayer, reading, and solitude.*

In other words, the most fulfilling moments often happen when our body or mind is pushed to its maximum capacity in a voluntary effort to achieve something challenging and meaningful. Interestingly, the tasks that can put us into flow are often more enjoyable than free time because they include built-in goals, feedback mechanisms, and challenges, all of which encourage engagement and concentration. In contrast, free time is unstructured and requires more effort to shape into something enjoyable. We thrive when deeply immersed in challenging activities. Aligning your life around the experience of flow, as inspired by Jesus' calling to live an abundant life, is a proven path to profound satisfaction.

When we lie on our deathbed, we will not be thinking of the number of likes we had on a post, but rather the tasks that required sacrifice and dedication—tasks that kept us completely engaged. Kim poignantly describes how these tasks are generally the ones that require sacrifice:

> Genuine joy comes alive in meaningful connection, not only to God the giver of joy but also to one another. We congratulate the birth of a child. Blood, sweat, tears that lead to joy. We congratulate the marriage of a couple. Time, energy, cost that lead to joy. We congratulate the graduation of a student. Sacrifice and discipline that lead to joy. This is what the blessed life looks like. Blood, sweat, tears, time, energy, cost, sacrifice, discipline—all leading to joy. It's a far cry from the cultural pursuit of happiness, where most attention is given to minimizing pain and maximizing pleasure. Though we expect the American ideal of the pursuit of happiness to lead us to joy, it is in fact struggle that leads to blessing, which then leads to joy. Feelings of happiness on the near side of the very real pain and struggle of life is a thin and flimsy set of pleasures. But when we travel through the very real pain and struggle of life, we discover blessing on the far side of the pain and struggle, undergirded and buoyed by the joy of the Lord.[46]

Finding Your Flow

To find your flow state, you need to choose one-to-three goals that align with your passions and allow you to further the kingdom of God in your own heart and/or in others. The goals should be meaningful to you and should push you to the edge of your abilities. You will know you have created these conditions and then entered a flow state because you will feel purely present in the moment and will have a loss of self-consciousness. You are like the little me who was lost in achieving the next level on the game.

For many of us, finding the tasks that further the kingdom of God and also align with our passions might be difficult at first. The disciplines described in this book—prayer, solitude, and reading—are all ways that we can develop our attention. Nature walks, journaling, serving others, and worship are all examples that might be a source for your flow state. Writing requires me to completely block out all distractions and focus completely. I will often go to a coffee shop to remove myself from the distractions at home and will dedicate a specified amount of time to writing. Deep reading is another example of a flow state I enjoy. Both of these allow me to focus deeply on one thing. Combined, both deep reading and the writing of this book have been transformative in helping my faith in God. And hopefully the writing of this book will help you grow in your faith.

Other examples of how you can integrate flow states into almost any area of your life include the following:

Flow at work: Distractions at work can seem, at times, impossible to control. Urgent emails and texts, interruptions from coworkers, and notifications on instant messaging are a few of the many ways we fail to focus. The good news is that you can build flow into any experience at your job.

Household activities: The tasks that you complete at home can be developed into flow states. These could be home improvement projects, cleaning, reading, playing an instrument, a painting or other form of artwork, a novel you have dreamed of writing, cooking a new dish with a recipe you have been excited to use, games for the family, creating or maintaining a garden, whittling, fishing, hiking, and reading deeply.

Exercise/Sports: Athletes report that when they're in a flow state, their movements seem effortless to them. The experience is generally described as a calmness related to other areas of life and an intense focus during the game. They also report a greater sense of control and confidence as they come to realize they are in the zone and doing well.[47]

Steps to Achieve Flow

Following are six critical steps that will help you identify activities in your life that will consistently put you into a state of flow and, therefore, minimize your distractions.

1. Start with Prayer

If you haven't already identified your flows, the first step is to dedicate time specifically to pray for and align yourself with God's guidance. Pray along with the psalmist, "In the morning, LORD, you hear my voice; in the morning I lay my requests before you and wait expectantly (Psalm 5:3)." Dietrich Bonhoeffer, a German pastor and anti-Nazi dissident, writes, "O God, early in the morning I cry to you. Help me to pray and to concentrate my thoughts on you; I cannot do this alone."[48]

Be sure you put the phone away, remove yourself from all distractions, and ask God to reveal or reconnect with you your passions. You will want to allow yourself time for reflection as part of your prayer. To help with this, you may want to even consider developing a mission statement or creed similar to the one in the opening of this chapter.

THE FOCUSED FAITH

Remember, you are seeking meaningful tasks in your life that will take the place of spending time tasks that don't lead to the abundant life.

2. Write out Your Goals

Long before our modern distractions, Arthur Bennett, in his classic book *How to Live on 24 Hours a Day* written in 1910, gives us a poignant reminder of how important a time of reflection can be to the abundant life:

> The exercise of concentrating the mind (to which at least half an hour a day should be given) is a mere preliminary, like scales on the piano. All the sensible people of all ages are agreed upon it. And it is not literature, nor is it any other art, nor is it history, nor is it any science. It is the study of one's self. Man, know thyself. I am entirely convinced that what is more than anything else lacking in the life of the average well-intentioned man of today is the reflective mood. We do not reflect. I mean that we do not reflect upon genuinely important things; upon the problem of our happiness, upon the main direction in which we are going, upon what life is giving to us, upon the share which reason has (or has not) in determining our actions, and upon the relation between our principles and our conduct. And yet you are in search of happiness, are you not? Have you discovered it? All I urge is that a life in which conduct does not fairly well accord with principles is a silly life; and that conduct can only be made to accord with principles by means of daily examination, reflection, and resolution.[49]

In researching this book, I had the pleasure of interviewing Jay Kim, author of *Analog Christian* and other books. As a pastor in Silicon Valley, he has thought and written extensively on how we can live out meaningful lives in the digital world. He even knew how to pronounce Csikszentmihalyi! While he offered multiple valuable insights, I especially appreciated his comments below on the importance of taking the time to individually reflect on the abundant life as Bennett described above, but from a Christian worldview:

> It's interesting when you think about how Csikszentmihalyi described the flow state. It's functionally in opposition to how we operate when we're scrolling. He talks about complete focus, almost like tunnel vision, where you are so engaged that you lose track of time and nothing else distracts you. In some ways, when we're scrolling, we also lose track of time, but it's because of distraction—we're just moving from one thing to the next. It's the opposite of focus. Online life does not require or demand anything of us; there's no skill required whatsoever. We've been led into this completely distracted state of being where it's hard to even answer what truly matters, because it's not an intellectual reality—you have to experience it to understand it. And that requires a focused flow.

To that end, I want to encourage you to set aside the time you need to remove distractions and make finding what truly matters for you an intellectual reality. Following are questions to consider as you endeavor this important task of brainstorming your existing flow activities or developing new ones:

> ❖ What activities have you done in the past where you lost track of time because you were so engaged?

> ❖ What skills or tasks do you enjoy that challenge you just enough—not too easy, but not overwhelming?

❖ When was the last time you felt completely absorbed in what you were doing? What were you doing?

❖ Do you have any hobbies or interests that require intense focus and attention?

❖ What type of tasks or projects make you feel a sense of accomplishment or satisfaction when completed?

❖ What activities allow you to use your strengths in a way that feels natural and rewarding?

❖ What are some tasks or activities that you look forward to and feel excited about starting?

❖ Which environments or settings make it easier for you to concentrate and stay focused?

❖ What activities do you find yourself naturally drawn to when you have free time?

❖ Have you ever experienced a sense of calm or clarity while doing a specific task? What was it, and how did it make you feel?

❖ Which activities make you feel more energized or refreshed even after you've spent a lot of time on them?

❖ Are there any repetitive tasks or routines that help you get into a rhythm or a focused state?

❖ What creative outlets allow you to express yourself fully and make you lose track of time?

❖ When working on something, do you prefer solitary focus or collaborative engagement. In which activities do you experience either of these?

❖ How can you incorporate more of the activities that make you feel "in the zone" into your daily or weekly routine?

Using the above questions, take the time to write out the specific goals you plan to achieve. Each of these goals should be stated clearly and, ideally, include the five parts of a SMART goal: Specific, Measurable, Attainable, Relevant, and Time-bound. In addition to clear objectives, it is critical that your goals have the elements needed to put you into a flow state: an appropriate challenge/skill balance and a feedback loop.

In addition to a clearly stated objective, flow states require a task that has an appropriate challenge/skill balance. Csikszentmihalyi called this the "flow channel."[50] It's commonly depicted in the way I've done in figure 1 below.

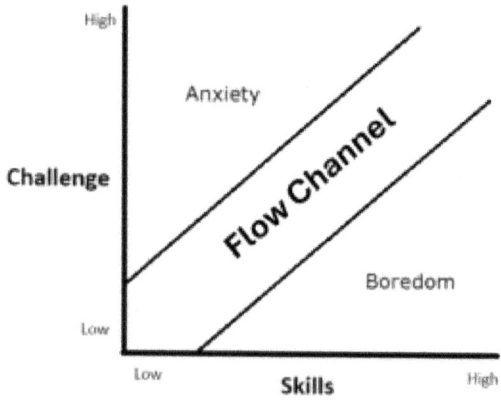

Figure 1: flow channel

THE FOCUSED FAITH 51

If the challenge for the task is too difficult, we slip into anxiety and ultimately failure. Conversely, if the task is too easy, we wallow in boredom. Between those two parameters, the task must require the optimal level of skills for you to complete the task. For example, if you are highly skilled, but a particular challenge is low, you'll get bored. The idea is to develop goals that are just beyond your current abilities yet achievable. Steven Kotler, in *The Rise of Superman: Decoding Science of Ultimate Human Performance*, found the optimal level of difficulty for a flow state. He suggests that the ideal challenge level is around 4 percent beyond the person's current abilities—enough to push the individual out of their comfort zone but not so much that it becomes overwhelming and induces anxiety.[51]

For example, imagine that you have just started to develop a running routine. Your current regimen averages three-to-five miles, five times per week. Then you decide to sign up for a marathon in one month. You commit to increasing your miles drastically over the next few weeks to train. The result is the task and deadline you selected will be too challenging unless you are naturally gifted in running. You will likely endure frustration and injuries due to the goal you selected, and it won't put you into a flow state. Conversely, if you decide to train for a one-mile fun run that takes place six months from now, the task will be too easy and you will likely become bored and, again, fail to get into the flow channel.

McGonigal, in *Reality is Broken: Why Games Make Us Better and How They Can Change the World*, discusses how gamification can be used to make tasks more engaging and how it can increase motivation by modifying the challenge level of tasks.[52] If the task you are completing is typically easy, consider using gamification to increase the challenge—for example, in the way I added a leaderboard and digital badges to online class discussions. Online discussions are, for many students, tedious and boring. By adding a leaderboard to the online discussion, the students worked both in teams and alone to increase their positions by creating additional posts and replies. Almost any tedious task can, with some thought, be gamified into a challenge that is appropriate. Fitness apps are another great example. I have personally benefited from creating challenges with friends that allow us to view each other's fitness over a specific time period.

Conversely, if the task you have selected seems too hard, you will want to consider breaking the task down into smaller but achievable milestones. For example, while training for a marathon in one month may not be the best goal for a beginner, it could be your goal if you register for a marathon a year from now and plan to first complete a 5K and then a half marathon.

3. *Identify a Baseline for Your Current Distraction Level*

Flow requires a feedback mechanism to allow you to know how you are performing. Since our smartphones provide a significant portion of the distractions in our routines, take the time to identify your current distraction level with your phone. Following are several questions and validated surveys to consider:

> ❖ Before you begin measuring your distraction level, without looking at your device, guess the answers to the following: How many times a day do I pick up my phone? How much time do I think I spend on my phone per day?

> ❖ Download a time-tracking app that will monitor how often and how long you are on your phone (time-tracking options might include Moment, Rescue Time, or ScreenTime).

❖ Over the course of five days, track how many times per day were you are on your phone and how much time you spend on your phone.

❖ Take the Smartphone Addiction Scale survey[1] to provide an assessment of your current smartphone usage.[53].

❖ Compare your data from the tracking app and surveys to your original guesses. How close were you? What if anything surprises you?

4. Develop and Follow a Pre-Flow Routine

We have all developed routines into our lives as a means to give our lives structure to support ourselves, the people around us, and the things in our lives we care about. We brush our teeth to support our long-term dental health. We perform certain tasks each day to help us wind down at night and prepare for the next day. The same is true for developing a flow routine. You need to develop a routine to ensure you incorporate it into your lifestyle and effectively mitigate distractions.

Following are several steps to help you develop a pre-flow routine:

❖ **Identify focus agents.** Write down activities that have helped you to focus in the past. For example, before dedicating time to writing at a coffee shop, I will sometimes go for a walk to pray and prepare my mind for the writing. Other times I will simply focus my thoughts on the task ahead with a silent car drive to the coffee shop. Other possibilities you might consider are listening to a specific type of music, praying in a particular way, reading inspirational material, or listening to a relevant podcast.

---

1. https://www.healthyscreens.com/scale

❖ **Eliminate external triggers.** Write down external triggers that help you to focus. I have personally benefited from working by myself in nature or working in a busy environment such as a coffee shop with background noise. I have also benefited from background instrumental worship or upbeat instrumental music. Others benefit from white noise such as that of a fan or a fountain. Others benefit from as much silence as possible.

❖ **Create a routine.** Using your notes from the first two steps, write down a specific routine you will use to help you prepare for your flow sessions. I encourage you to experiment with several examples, and if one method starts to fail, be willing to experiment with another method for a while.

❖ **Create a distraction-free environment.** Flow requires an environment in which we will not be distracted. By definition, flow requires that we give the task our complete attention. Therefore, we need to take the time to ensure external distractions are minimized. Small changes can yield big results in terms of triggering a flow state. I have personally benefited from using the do-not-disturb function on my phone, wearing headphones with instrumental music, closing my office door, and letting family know in advance of the need to focus for a specified time period.

5: Create a Feedback Loop

The fifth area to consider is the feedback loop. When you enter into a flow state, you have a clear goal that has an appropriate challenge/skill balance, and you receive regular feedback. Gamers, while in a flow state, have a clear goal for the game and a constant feedback mechanism in terms of points related to other players and/or levels attained.

For example, the feedback loop in a goal to run a marathon in one year is your weekly goals. Generally, the rule for running is to avoid training more than 10 percent beyond your current activity level. Thus, a well-defined feedback mechanism is a plan that gradually increases your miles by 10 percent over the course of the year. As you attain each weekly and monthly milestone, your confidence grows about your ability to attain your goal.

6. *Commit to Monotasking*

Flow requires a commitment to completing one task at a time. The planning you completed in the previous steps to developing a pre-flow routine and removing external distractions will set the stage for you to focus on your goal. Our culture seems to put great value in multitasking, but the reality and growing research is that simultaneously completing multiple tasks requiring a degree of attention is less productive and effective than monotasking.[54]

The reality is that it takes time for most people to build their comfort and train their brain to monotask. In order to build your endurance in this, start small and work up to longer periods. First, define and develop blocking time in your day. Practice a single task for a short block of time and then allow yourself a short break. For example, start with setting a timer to focus on a particular task for ten minutes, then allow yourself a two-minute break. Over time, you will develop the ability to lengthen your monotasking timeframe—from ten to twenty minutes, to one hour, and even two hours. A similar and popular technique is the Pomodoro method, in which you work in twenty-five-minute intervals with five minute breaks.

Csikszentmihalyi has said that individuals in flow can sustain attention for several hours if the challenge and skill level are appropriate.[55] I have personally found that, during writing or research, I can commit to monotasking and easily enter a flow state in which I am completely focused on the task. However, the internal commitment to focus exclusively on the task requires intense mental resources, and I generally need a break after a maximum of four hours.

In the end, it is up to you to decide what timeframe feels realistic for you to devote your complete attention. Start small and be kind to yourself as you build your tolerance for monotasking.

Application Guide

Discover how to enter and maintain a 'flow state' with practical exercises in the Application Guide. Visit here[2]. You'll find practical steps to begin reclaiming your focus.

---

2. https://www.thefocusedfaith.com/free

THE FOCUSED FAITH

Key Points

❖ The abundant life is achieved by focusing on what truly matters, not by managing distractions.

❖ Flow states, where one is fully engaged, are essential to experiencing true joy and fulfillment.

❖ Focus on what truly matters in your life rather than simply managing distractions.

❖ Pursue activities that bring you into a flow state, where you are fully engaged and experience true joy.

❖ Identify and dedicate time to meaningful tasks that align with your God-given purpose.

Questions for Reflection

1. Read Matthew 13:44–46. What treasures in your life are being overlooked because of digital distractions? How can you "sell everything" to pursue what truly matters?

2. How does focusing on meaningful activities help you experience the abundant life Jesus offers? Consider an example from your own life.

3. What are the passions or activities that demand your full attention? How can you incorporate more of these into your daily routine?

Screens and Souls: How Technology Shapes Our Walk with God

For where your treasure is, there your heart will be also.

–Matthew 6:21

One of the great uses of Twitter and Facebook will be to prove at the Last Day that prayerlessness was not from lack of time.

–John Piper

Douglas Adams, author of *The Hitchhiker's Guide to the Galaxy*, grouped technology into three categories. First, everything that's already in the world when you were born is just normal. Second, anything invented between then and when you turn thirty is incredibly exciting and creative. Finally, anything invented after you're thirty is against the natural order of things and the beginning of the end of civilization as we know it—until it's been around for about ten years when it gradually becomes alright.[56]

Our perceptions of technology change, as do our concerns. John Dyer explains succinctly, "Rather than taking our cues about technology from the scriptures and the outline of God's plan for humanity, we seem to be locked in a cycle of questioning the really new but accepting the just barely old."[57] The battle for your attention is not won solely by offensively building a life full of flow activities. It must also be won defensively by developing a biblical worldview of technology.

We all have a worldview. Here is how John Sire defines worldview in *The Universe Next Door*: "Worldview is a framework or a set of fundamental beliefs through which we view the world and our calling in it."

Instead of seeing Christianity and technology as intersecting slightly, we need to view technology through a biblical lens, allowing the Bible to shape our view of technology.

Ephesians 5:8–10 says, "You were once darkness, but now you are light in the Lord. Live as children of light (for the fruit of the light consists in all goodness, righteousness and truth) and find out what pleases the Lord." Our role as Christians living in this digital age is to "find out what is acceptable to the Lord" in relation to the impact of technology on our lives and respond accordingly. To do this, we cannot leave technology as an unexamined aspect of our lives. To begin, let's answer a fundamentally simple question:

What Is Technology?

Consider a smartphone and a pen. Which of these is an example of technology? In truth, almost all the tools we use daily—cars, televisions, even ballpoint pens—were invented in the past 150 years. Today, these tools are so normal that it seems strange to call them technology. Computer scientist Alan Kay, who played a significant role in the development of windows, is often attributed as saying, "We tend to define technology as anything that was invented after you were born." The word technology consists of two parts: *tekne*, which means craft, skill, or art, and *logea*, which refers to the systematic study of a subject. Dyer combines both of these with the following definition. *Technology:* The human activity of using tools to transform God's creation for practical purposes.[58]

Whether it is creating a computer program to solve a problem, a spreadsheet to build a budget, or using AI to create images from text, we use our tools daily to transform God's creation for practical purposes.

The Effects of Technology

In almost every course I have taught, I ask my students to interact with the following statement I adapted from Dyer's book: "One of the most dangerous things you can believe is that technology is neutral."[59]

Take a moment to develop your opinion on this important statement. Agree or Disagree?

Many of my students initially disagree, arguing that technology, like the argument against gun control, is a tool entirely dependent on how it is used by the user. Or do the technologies we use every day, including our devices, have a transformative effect on our lives regardless of how we decide to use them? As it turns out, this argument has been studied for many years from a spectrum of technological views ranging from determinism to instrumentalism.

Determinism is the notion that all events, including our decisions and behaviors, are guided by something in their past. In this view, our lives are just a series of chain reactions, one event leading to another without real significance because everything has already been preordained by past events. For example, in the attention economy, determinism could argue that we are so predictable that our online behaviors can be reduced to algorithms that control how we spend our time daily. According to this mindset, there is no place for free will or personal decision-making because everything happens according to a pre-set program.

On the other hand, instrumentalism takes a more practical approach, focusing on how useful something is rather than on how true it is. In the context of technology, instrumentalism suggests that we use tools, such as apps or social media, to accomplish specific goals rather than being controlled by them. For Christians navigating the attention economy, instrumentalism means treating technology as tools that can be used to enhance our spiritual lives, such as using apps to pray or stay connected with our church community. Instead of letting technology control us, we can make it work for our benefit.

Soft determinism, also known as compatibilism, tries to find a balance between the strict control of determinism and the freedom of instrumentalism. It acknowledges that our actions can be influenced by external forces, like algorithms or notifications designed to keep us engaged, but it also believes that we still have some degree of free will. For Christians, this means recognizing that while the attention economy might pull us in certain directions, we still have the power to choose how we spend our time and focus on what truly matters, like prayer, worship, and serving others.

When we compare these three ideas, we see that they each offer a different perspective on how much control we have over our actions in the attention economy. Determinism suggests that we have very little control because everything is already determined by past events. Instrumentalism emphasizes how we can use technology as a tool to achieve our goals, putting us in control. Soft determinism offers a compromise, acknowledging that while we are influenced by external forces, we still retain some choice. For Christians, these ideas can help us think about how we interact with the digital world and whether we are being led by technology or leading our own lives with purpose. Once we become aware of the transformative effects of technology on our lives, we can take action to mitigate its effects on our lives in areas like solitude, prayer, and reading.

THE FOCUSED FAITH

How Are You Being Shaped?

Samuel James writes, "The question is not, is this technology shaping me right now? The question is, how is this technology shaping me right now?"[60] John Dyer uses an example of a shovel to illustrate the power of technology to transform. Initially, he writes the shovel seems neutral, capable of both good and bad uses. However, using the shovel also transforms the person using it—causing blisters, calluses, and sore muscles. Thus, the shovel and every other formal technology has both intentional and unintentional effects. For example, during the pandemic, our church used Zoom to continue meeting virtually. Post-pandemic, we allowed virtual attendance but eventually decided to return to in-person meetings for deeper connections. While meeting virtually via zoom served a purpose, it also had limitations.

John reminds us of this in his writings: "I have much to write to you, but I do not want to use paper and ink. Instead, I hope to visit you and talk with you face to face, so that our joy may be complete" 2 John 1:12.

Whether using pen and paper or meeting virtually via Zoom meetings, we transform God's creation with our tools, but these tools also transform us.

Transformation in History

When we look at our history, we see clear examples of how technology that was once deemed neutral transformed us and those living in the world at that time. In *Understanding Media: The Extensions of Man*, Marshall McLuhan illustrates how advances in building the railroads and the airplane both created different worlds to support the tools.[61] It's not simply that jet airliners travel thousands of miles because that's what we want them to do. Both of these tools transformed how each the individuals living in that time viewed themselves and their place in the world. Similarly, Henry Ford's assembly line did not just give us a "neutral" tool that allowed many more people to travel easier. It also transformed the options that our world had in regard to where to work. Prior to these tools, the thought of travelling hundreds or thousands of miles away from home for a short period of time wasn't even an option.

Nicholas Carr, in *The Shallows*, summarizes McLuhan's work and the argument of technology as neutral, saying,

> When people start debating (as they always do) whether the medium's effects are good or bad, it's the content they wrestle over. What both enthusiast and skeptic miss is what McLuhan saw: that in the long run a medium's content matters less than the medium itself in influencing how we think and act. As our window onto the world, and onto ourselves, a popular medium molds what we see and how we see it.[62]

Cognitive Drift: The Shaping Influence of AI

Carr's book was groundbreaking for bringing awareness of the how the internet could shape our minds. Today, Artificial Intelligence (AI) is presenting an even more powerful example of a formidable force that shapes not only how we live but also how we think, reason, and engage with the world around us. For Christians, this transformation presents both unique challenges and profound spiritual implications.

The advent of artificial intelligence represents a significant shift in how we interact with information. When Carr wrote his book in 2010, he correctly pointed out that the internet was shaping our ability to engage in deep reading. But we were still engaging our attention as we actively sought out knowledge, sifting through search results, reading articles, and forming our own conclusions. Today, AI offers to streamline this process, delivering pre-packaged answers, essays, and even entire manuscripts.

Large language models are just one type of artificial intelligence that, at the time of this writing, consist of platforms such as OpenAI's GPT series, Google's Bard (PaLM) and Gemini, and Microsoft's Pilot. I attended a technology conference in which the keynote speakers, CEOs, and CIOs of from these companies and others discussed the exciting possibilities for these technologies including dramatic productivity gains and even bold predictions that certain diseases would be cured in the next three years. I am among the vast majority of the world who shares this excitement and have even grown to rely on the tools myself for helping organize research, writing, and trivial tasks like finding a good recipe. However, on my flight home, my thoughts returned to this book and a critical question: *What happens to our cognitive abilities when we no longer need to engage deeply with the information we consume?*

As Christians, we are called to "renew our minds" (Romans 12:2), a process that requires active engagement with Scripture, prayer, and reflection. Yet as AI begins to handle more of our mental tasks, from decision-making to problem-solving, we risk losing our capacity for deep thought, reflection, and spiritual discernment. The Bible warns against the dangers of laziness and complacency (Proverbs 19:15; 24:30–34), and there is a real danger that the convenience offered by AI could lead us down a path of mental and spiritual atrophy.

The attention economy thrives on our engagement, often manipulating our choices and subtly influencing our decisions. We have all grown used to, and even love, the AI systems like Netflix's recommended movie, which suggest products based on our preferences or, more likely, on sponsored content. These systems are shaping my own ability to make decisions, increasingly outsourcing the decisions to machines that predict my desires and preferences with uncanny accuracy.

This loss of agency is particularly concerning for Christians, who believe in the God-given gift of free will. Our ability to choose right from wrong and to seek God's will in our lives is central to our faith. When we allow AI to make decisions on our behalf, we risk diminishing our capacity for moral and spiritual discernment. The Bible reminds us that "humans plan their course, but the LORD establishes their steps" (Proverbs 16:9). Yet in an AI-driven world, the steps we take may no longer be guided by our own hearts and minds, but by algorithms designed to maximize engagement and profit.

While it is too early to see the long-term effects of how this technology is shaping our lives, we can look to history to see how similar advances effected our cognitive abilities. Studies have shown that reliance on technology, such as GPS for navigation or the internet for information retrieval, can diminish our natural cognitive abilities.[63] One study found the more dependent we become on GPS for our navigation, the worse our navigation abilities become.[64] I can definitely relate. In the early days of my work in the tech world, I travelled every week using *Thomas Guide* maps and became quite good at navigating a new state each week and finding my way around the city. Today I feel the cognitive shift in my spatial awareness and sense of direction as I have grown completely reliant on my navigation system. So the looming question for our day is this: *If GPS has dramatically altered our brain's ability to navigate, what will AI do to our brain's ability to focus, create, and analyze the world around us?*

As we navigate this new landscape, it is crucial for Christians to remain vigilant. The convenience and efficiency offered by AI are tempting, but we must resist the urge to relinquish our cognitive and spiritual agency completely. Instead, we should seek to engage deeply with the world around us, using technology as a tool rather than a crutch. In practical terms, this means being intentional about how we use AI and other digital tools. It means setting aside time for reflection, prayer, and study, without the constant intrusion of AI-generated content. It means cultivating the discipline to engage in deep thinking, even when it is easier to let AI do the work for us.

A Biblical Worldview on Tech

Given the power of all these digital technologies to mold and shape us, how are we to respond with a biblical worldview of technology? The answer for many Christians is to avoid the temptations of pornography, anti-Christian content, and strive to use the internet for good. Unfortunately, while we should certainly do these things, this answer falls short. This is because a biblical worldview should not simply be about using neutral tools in right ways versus wrong ways because the tools themselves influence how we perceive reality. When our tools not only change our experience of God's world but also distort it, they can become something more than tools—they become idols.

Samuel James reminds us that rather than being a neutral tool, the internet (particularly the social internet) is an epistemological environment—a spiritual and intellectual habitat—that creates in its members particular ways of thinking, feeling, and believing. Rather than thinking of the web and social media as merely neutral tools that merely do whatever users ask of them, it is better to think of them as kinds of spaces that are continually shaping us to think, feel, communicate, and live in certain ways.[65]

We influence technology, but technology also influences us. Different technologies have different impacts on us. The digital devices we carry and frequently check throughout the day are molding us into specific types of thinkers, with thought patterns shaped by these technologies.

We didn't consciously choose the digital world we're now part of; we seem to have ended up here almost by accident. These technologies increasingly determine our behaviors and emotions, often compelling us to use them more than we believe is healthy, sometimes at the expense of more meaningful activities. We often feel a loss of control—like when we pull out our phones during a conversation or feel the urge to document a moment rather than simply enjoying it.

People don't become addicted to screens solely due to a lack of discipline. As we've already established, immense resources have been invested to make this outcome likely. We were steered into this digital landscape by influential tech companies and the attention economy, which discovered enormous profits in a gadget-and app-dominated culture. As Tristan Harris highlights, "Are apps being programmed, or are people being programmed? They are programming people. The narrative that technology is neutral and that it's up to us to choose how we use it is misleading. These technologies are designed to be engaging and used for long durations to maximize profit."[66]

Application Guide

To evaluate your relationship with technology and its impact on your spiritual life, check out the 'Technology and Your Walk with God Checklist' in the Application Guide here[1] or by visiting here[2]. You'll find practical steps to begin reclaiming your focus today.

Key Points

---

1. https://www.thefocusedfaith.com/free
2. https://www.thefocusedfaith.com/free

❖ Technology is not neutral; it shapes our perceptions and actions.

❖ Developing a biblical worldview of technology is essential to avoid being led astray.

❖ Examine how your current use of technology aligns or conflicts with your values.

❖ Be intentional in your choices of technology to ensure it supports your spiritual growth.

Questions for Reflection

1. Read Matthew 6:21. How does this verse relate to your current relationship with technology? What practical steps can you take to ensure your "treasure" aligns with God's kingdom?

2. How has technology influenced your spiritual practices both positively and negatively? Consider ways to mitigate the negative impacts.

3. What does it mean to view technology through a biblical lens? How can this perspective help you navigate the digital age?

Alone, Not Lonely: The Transformative Gift of Solitude

Jesus often withdrew to lonely places and prayed.

–Luke 5:16

Conversation enriches the understanding,

but solitude is the school of genius.

–Edward Gibbon

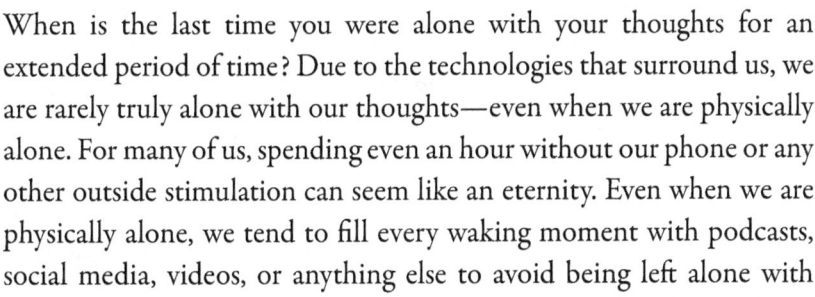

When is the last time you were alone with your thoughts for an extended period of time? Due to the technologies that surround us, we are rarely truly alone with our thoughts—even when we are physically alone. For many of us, spending even an hour without our phone or any other outside stimulation can seem like an eternity. Even when we are physically alone, we tend to fill every waking moment with podcasts, social media, videos, or anything else to avoid being left alone with ourselves.

To test just how far we will go to avoid being alone, University of Virginia psychologist Tim Wilson and Harvard's Dan Gilbert, conducted research on fifty-five undergrads. Each college student was asked to go into a windowless, unassuming room with simple furniture designed to minimize any outside stimulation. Once inside the room, they were exposed to various types of stimuli such as music and pictures and even mild electric shocks. When the researchers then asked if they would pay to avoid being shocked the vast majority—forty-two out of forty-five—said they would pay to avoid the shock. The crazy part of this study is that after this conversation, each student was told to spend the next fifteen minutes "just thinking." However, if desired, they could press a button to give themselves a shock. Astonishingly, one third of the men and one fourth of the women who said they would pay to avoid getting shocked gave themselves a shock to avoid being left alone with their thoughts. One participant even shocked himself 190 times![67]

A Modern Example

John Mark Comer, pastor of Bridgetown Church in Portland, Oregon, is a leader in helping others learn the importance of solitude. His website, practicingtheway.org, has a video in which he asks us to consider, "What if the greatest threat to the Christian faith today isn't secularism but distraction?" Author of *The Ruthless Elimination of Hurry*, Comer explains that like so many of us, his journey toward solitude began after experiencing burnout from the hectic pace of ministry and the constant demands of modern technology.[68]

Inspired by the example of Jesus, Comer made several changes to his life. First, he designed his schedule to incorporate regular periods of solitude into his daily routine. Once the schedule was set, he began to set strict boundaries around the use of his digital devices to ensure they did not encroach on his time of solitude and prayer. Through these practices, Comer's life was transformed in a way that allowed him to slow down, reconnect with God and find a deeper meaning and purpose in life.

In our hyperconnected world, technology offers unprecedented convenience, connectivity, and entertainment; however, amidst the relentless digital noise, the practice of solitude—a crucial aspect of spiritual and personal growth—has become increasingly rare. This chapter explores the biblical importance of solitude, the perils of technology in creating solitude deprivation, and how we can reclaim technology to foster a life that embraces solitude.

Biblical Mandate for Solitude

The Bible offers countless examples of the importance of solitude, especially with Jesus. While Jesus did not have to contend with the same distractions we have in the digital age, we learn from his life the importance of solitude in the many ways he escaped the distractions of his ministry: the crowds, the enemy, and disciples. We see Him embracing solitude as a means to prepare for the events in His such as the forty days in the wilderness preparing for the temptation from the enemy (Luke 4:1–2) and in the final moments before the cross in Gethsemane (Matthew 26:36–46). We see Him using solitude as a means to restore Himself when he "went up on a mountainside by Himself to pray" (Matthew 14:23) and before choosing His twelve disciples (Luke 6:12–13) and after performing miracles (Mark 1:35).

While we need look no further than Jesus' life, Elijah and David also offer more examples of the power of this important practice. Elijah's forty days and nights of solitude on Mount Horeb (1 Kings 19:4–13) provided the space for hearing that still, small voice in guiding his next steps. David's psalms, such as Psalm 23 and Psalm 62, exemplify both why and how his life was filled with the peace and trust that comes with contemplation, worship, and time alone with God.

Combined, we see the Bible paint a picture of men and women who embraced solitude, not simply as a means to avoid distraction, but also as a deliberate method of contemplation, reflection, renewal, and engaging deeply with God.

Solitude in Leadership

Jesus' example of leadership is our most powerful example of the power of solitude in our spiritual lives. But what is the role of solitude in leadership for business and other areas of life? It turns out that the greatest leaders in the world have created solitude as a critical part of their lives. Anthony Storr, in *Solitude: A Return to the Self*, describes how great thinkers such as Descartes and Nietzsche thrived on solitude.[69] Benjamin Franklin, one of the American founders, wrote in his journal, "I acknowledge solitude as an agreeable refreshment to a busy mind."[70] Abraham Lincoln, for example, used his time alone to reflect upon the pressures of the Civil War and navigate the immense pressures of his presidency. His "Meditation on the Divine Will," written in 1862, reflects his deep introspection and reliance on solitude for spiritual and mental clarity during challenging times.[71] Biographer David Garrow writes that Martin Luther King Jr. attributes the "most important night of [King's]" life as a night he spent alone in silence and prayer. It was during this time God gave profoundly changed his view of his ministry and gave him immense courage to fight for justice and truth.[72]

In more recent years, we can look to the examples of solitude found in the founders of Fortune 500 companies. Steve Wozniak, cofounder of Apple, wrote in his memoir that the best inventions are often the result of solitary work, free from the influence of committees and teams. He wrote, "Most inventors and engineers I've met are like me—they're shy and they live in their heads. They're almost like artists. In fact, the very best of them are artists. And artists work best alone—best outside of corporate environments, best where they can control an invention's design without a lot of other people designing it for marketing or some other committee. I don't believe anything really revolutionary has ever been invented by committee. Work alone. Not on a committee. Not on a team."[73]

THE FOCUSED FAITH

Bill Gates, founder of Microsoft, was known for his "Think Weeks," in which he would dedicate two weeks per year to seclude himself to read and think deeply about his life and company. Gates championed these times alone to others, especially introverts, as a secret weapon that allows for deep focus on complex issues.[74]

In an essay for the *Harvard Business Review* titled "Executives, Protect Your Alone Time," the authors point to the importance of solitude in business. They point out that, while artists have always understood the importance of solitude to the creative process, there is new science (which we will go into more in a later chapter) that shows it's vital for developing creativity in business too.[75]

Despite the countless examples we could continue to identify, along with the underlying yearning we all have at times for solitude, why do we continue to struggle with finding time alone? I believe the answer lies, at least in part, in the role of technology in our lives.

Solitude Deprivation

Cal Newport, author of *Deep Work* and *Digital Minimalism* has coined a phenomenon most of us have lived with to one degree or another: solitude deprivation. He defines this as "a state in which you spend close to zero time alone with your thoughts and free from input from other minds."[76] While our technology offers innumerable options to connect us, it can impede our ability to experience true solitude. Matthew Crawford has gone as far to say that silence is a scarce resource in today's loud world in which we need to survive. Just as air makes breathing possible, silence makes it possible for us to think.[77]

There are multiple causes for our current state of solitude deprivation. However, the research seems to indicate at least four significant causes:

constant connectivity, the prevalence of digital distractions, FOMO (fear of missing out), and the addictive nature of our tools.

Constant Connectivity

First, our smartphones have centered us in a world in which we are constantly connected to outside stimulation, leaving little-to-no room for uninterrupted solitude. Unfortunately, the research is showing that the problem is getting worse every year. In my review, I found that, in 2018, the average smartphone user unlocked their phone eighty times per day.[78] In 2024, smartphone owners on average unlocked their phones 150 times per day,[79] and over 50 percent of cell phone users never switch off their phones. Clearly, our phones provide the benefit of immediate gratification, but they erode, and continue to, erode our tolerance for stillness and the benefits that come with prolonged focus and solitude.

Prevalence of Digital Distractions

Second, the mere presence of a smartphone can significantly reduce cognitive capacity and attention span. Researchers have found that a smartphone within reach, even if it is turned off, can still occupy our cognitive resources, and impair our ability to focus fully.[80] Most often, however, our phones are not off when we are alone, and our notifications, updates, and messages fragment our attention when we are left alone with our thoughts. A study by Gloria Mark, professor of informatics at the University of California, Irvine, found that it takes an average of twenty-three minutes and fifteen seconds to return to a task after an interruption.[81] The concept of "attention residue" also explains why digital notifications are so disruptive. According to research by Sophie Leroy, a professor at the University of Washington, attention residue occurs when part of our attention remains focused on the previous task, making it difficult to fully engage in a new task.[82] This means that every notification or digital interruption leaves a residue, reducing the quality of our focus and diminishing the potential for deep thought and reflection.

Fear of Mission Out (FOMO)

Third, the feeling of FOMO, Fear of Missing Out, created by today's social media drives us to pick up our phone and stay online and engaged. Fortunately, in recent years, I have noticed a willingness—and even hunger—from those around me to detox from social media, either temporarily or indefinitely. I believe more people are personally experiencing, and becoming aware of the research, that the very platforms designed to connect us are leading to feelings of social isolation. Jay Kim, writes, "We are compelled to continue scrolling and liking until finally we turn in on ourselves, wondering why our real lives don't look, sound, and feel like others' filtered images; even worse, we lose sense of real life, and our real selves, leading to self-centric despair."[83] The research supports our feelings and shows that heavy use of social media ultimately leads us to greater feelings of isolation from others. Users who spend more than two hours a day on social media are twice as likely to experience perceived social isolation than those who spend a half hour or less. Heavy social media users, who visit sites fifty-eight or more times a week, are three times as likely to experience perceived social isolation than those who visit minimally at nine times or less a week.[84] This paradox of the promise for social media to connect highlights the need for us to learn to follow the example of our savior and intentionally embrace solitude in order to cultivate genuine connections.

Addictive Nature of Our Tools

Finally, as we have established already, our attention economy has made us physically addicted to our phones. If you have ever attempted to do a digital fast or digital detox, you know the familiar feeling that comes when we are separated from our devices. My pastor has termed this sensation as our need for our next "dopamine cookie." Dopamine, as we learned before, is the neurotransmitter that records experiences in our brain as pleasurable and prompts us to repeat them. This chemical plays a central role in the desire for sex and drugs, yet it also functions similarly in the desire we have for swiping and tapping our phones, especially during times of solitude.

Reclaiming Technology and Embracing Solitude

While the attention economy, dopamine, and our devices certainly work against our ability to spend time alone, the good news is it doesn't have to be that way. The fact you are reading this is bringing you awareness of the problem, which is the first step in solving it. One of my biggest goals for this book is to raise awareness of these issues to allow you to begin to take steps to change your life.

To counteract solitude deprivation, we must intentionally evaluate the technology in our lives and use it to support rather than hinder our spiritual and personal growth. Following are several practical challenges for you to consider to achieve this balance:

Create Space for Solitude

Proactively decide when and where you will allow tech in your life. Andy Crouch, in *Tech Wise Family*, suggests a goal of 1-1-1: Remove tech from your life for one hour per day, one day per week, and one week per year.[85] Practically, this might translate to a "no phone zone" for the one hour around the table each day at dinner, a "digital sabbath on Sunday," and a week each year, probably a vacation, in which tech is removed from our lives.

One hour per day. I am an introvert by nature. So for me solitude is something I crave—though I admit that finding the discipline to tame my tech to allow me this time has been difficult. An approach that works well for me is to carve out time alone each day during my devotional time, morning run or walk, driving time, and occasional weekend retreats. I have found that if I can avoid the temptation to look at my phone the first thing in morning (even for texts), my day goes much smoother, and I am much happier.

Research supports this, showing that we only have three hours of peak mental performance, and that morning is generally best.[86] However, looking at our phones the first thing in the morning can activate stress responses, such as an adrenaline release, and adversely affect the rest of your day. One study found that early morning exposure to digital screens can increase cortisol levels, leading to heightened stress and anxiety throughout the day.[87] So even though I generally use an app on my phone for my morning devotion, I have tried to ensure that I always start with my time in the Word of God followed by prayer. After an hour or so (and a few cups of coffee), I will allow emails and texts back into my life and take on the day. Another approach that has worked well for me is incorporating an hour walk or run into the day. While I may listen to a podcast or music, I have tried to ensure I spend at least twenty-to-thirty minutes of this time alone with my thoughts and in prayer.

Turning off the radio and refusing to look or listen to my phone during my drives has opened up a whole new, previously untapped, time of solitude. At first, this took some getting used to. I found myself getting bored and desperately wanting to fill the silence with the radio, my podcasts, or music. Now I highly value the time alone and find it critical to thinking about what lies ahead for me at my next destination that day or much further in life.

One or more days a week/year. I have tried to set aside time at least quarterly to spend one-to-two entire days in solitude. The simplest approach for me is to plan for a day at the beach or mountains and intentionally fast from my phone and other tech. Some of my most treasured times alone have been when I have been able to do this for multiple days. Whether it is camping at the beach or spending time alone in a mountain cabin, I find these weekend retreats incredibly life changing, and without fail they provide the refreshment and perspective I need to move forward in life.

Tame Your Tech

Aside from setting aside times in your life for solitude, we can "tame our tech" to protect our solitude. There are many ways to accomplish this and we will discuss them more in future chapters. For now, consider these challenges:

Silence or remove your notifications. Take the time to silence or, preferably, remove all of your notifications. This small change was a game changer in my life. The simple presence of an incoming email alert on my phone could derail my focus or time alone or with family. I use the focus settings in iPhone to remove all notifications and incoming text messages. This valuable feature gives you full control over the apps you want to allow to interrupt your life.

Put your phone away at home. Cal Newport, in *Digital Minimalism*, suggests simply putting your phone away while you are at home. This is one that I continue to find a challenge. I did try this approach, and it was difficult for me. Newport's simple but powerful argument is that we really don't need to carry our phones with us all the time, especially at home. In addition to creating space when we don't use our phones at all, like the one hour per day, this idea is the reverse: Create space in your day when you *do* use your phone at home. Put the phone away in a drawer or plugged in at your office. Designate a specific time, or times, each day that you will allow yourself to interact with others on your phone. This simple change can unlock much more time for you and your thoughts at home that would have been previously filled with mindless scrolling.

Measure your tech. One of my favorite sayings, reportedly from the management theorist Peter Drucker, is, "What gets measured gets improved." This is especially true for our tech. By regularly assessing your digital habits and their impact on your well-being, you can identify areas where technology use may be hindering your solitude, and you can make adjustments as needed. Self-assessment promotes awareness and intentionality in managing digital engagement. To do this, start by deciding to weekly monitor your phone's screen time, and set goals to reduce the time you spend on mindless activities. Apps like Moment, Screen Time (for iOS), Digital Wellbeing (for Android), Forest, and RescueTime can help you curb the amount of time you spend on your phone. These apps offer features such as tracking usage, setting limits, providing insights, and even gamifying the process of staying off your phone to promote healthier digital habits.

Moment tracks how much time you spend on your phone and helps you set daily limits to reduce usage. Screen Time is built into iOS devices and provides detailed reports on your device usage and allows you to set daily limits for specific apps. Digital Wellbeing for Android devices tracks usage, sets app limits, and includes features like Wind Down to reduce screen time before bed. Forest is a unique app that helps you stay focused by planting virtual trees that grow as you stay off your phone, promoting a sense of accomplishment and mindfulness. RescueTime offers detailed insights into your digital habits, helps set goals, and provides alerts to help you stay focused.

Get Accountable

Engage with a community that values and practices solitude. You can do this by sharing your goals and desires for accountability with family, friends and church members asking them to keep you accountable.

Journaling

Maintain a journal to document your experiences with solitude and digital disconnection; reflect on the challenges, insights, and spiritual growth that occur during these periods.

Conclusion

In a world dominated by technology, embracing solitude requires intentionality and discipline; by following biblical examples and setting mindful boundaries, we can reclaim technology's role in our lives, transforming it from a source of distraction to a tool that enhances our spiritual journey. Solitude, when nurtured, becomes a wellspring of strength, clarity, and connection with God, leading to a truly abundant life. Embracing solitude in the digital age is not about rejecting technology but about using it wisely and purposefully to support our spiritual and personal growth. Through intentional practices, we can cultivate a balanced digital life that honors the value of solitude and fosters a deeper connection with God, with our own minds, and with others.

Application Guide

Learn how to carve out intentional solitude in your life through practical strategies in the Application Guide here[1]. You'll find practical steps to begin reclaiming your focus today.and start experiencing the clarity and peace that solitude offers.

---

1. https://www.thefocusedfaith.com/free

Key Points

❖ Solitude is crucial for spiritual growth, but it is increasingly rare in a hyperconnected world.

❖ Make solitude a regular practice in your life in order to foster spiritual growth.

❖ Recognize and combat solitude deprivation by carving out time for intentional, tech-free reflection.

❖ Implement practical steps like daily digital fasts to incorporate solitude into your routine.

Questions for Reflection

1 Read Luke 5:16. How did Jesus use solitude in His ministry, and how can you follow His example in your own life?

2. In what ways has technology created "solitude deprivation" in your life? How can you reclaim moments of solitude for spiritual growth?

3. Recall a time when solitude led to a significant spiritual or personal breakthrough. How can you prioritize solitude in your daily routine?

Focused Hearts, Open Souls: Attention and Prayer

Be still and know that I am God.

−Psalm 46:10

I'm a big believer in boredom. . . . All the [tech] stuff is wonderful, but having nothing to do can be wonderful, too.

−Steve Jobs

❖

Unlike most people, I love and look forward to a long-haul flight. I have been blessed to lead students on multiple international trips, and before that I was required to travel extensively for work. I love watching people on these flights and simply observing how those around me respond to multiple hours of life in "airplane mode." For most people, they will do anything to pass this time quickly. On a nine-hour flight to Europe, I did an informal research project of my own and mentally tracked how passengers used this time. From my informal observations, activities that are most popular while in literal airplane mode are, in order: (1) sleeping, (2) watching movies, (3) playing games, (4) reading, (5) working, and (6) having conversations with others. Rarely do I ever notice anyone on a plane—or anywhere else really—who is simply present or in thought. Moreover, it seems that we as a culture have actually grown uncomfortable with situations in which we are the ones hiding behind a screen while someone else in our midst is simply present or in deep thought.

I know this because I am generally one of these individuals who sits next to you and is not buried in a device. I have come to cherish the long-haul flight because it is one of the very few places left in the world where I am forced to disconnect from all incoming distractions for a significant period of time. This uninterrupted time allows me to dive deep into my thoughts. Typically, I will make a mental list of several concerns at work or in the family, and then instead of filling the time with another bad movie, I work through these issues in my mind, using prayer and introspection. I have *never* been disappointed for making this decision, and it has led to some of the biggest breakthroughs in my life, including career changes, a new perspective on a family problem, or just a newly found peace that God is in control. Similarly, my morning runs provide a comparable sanctuary. Just like being on a long flight, running leaves me alone with my thoughts, away from the distractions of daily life. I spent weeks thinking about a title for this book. Then during a run, the title just came to me out of the blue.

C. S. Lewis said, "My morning thoughts are like a thousand wild animals" clamoring for attention.[88] Attentiveness is one of the most difficult concepts to grasp but one of the most valuable to learn. As distractible people living in a very distracting world, Lewis's metaphor captures the challenge many of us face in our spiritual lives: Our technology, our own thoughts, and the world around us all compete for our attention from the moment we wake.

Our prayer lives are not immune from distractions in our lives. Think about the last time you had a very intense and powerful moment of prayer, when you clearly felt and heard from God. For the vast majority of us, it has become increasingly rare.

This chapter invites you to relearn to pray by studying the three varieties of attention: focused, rote, and boredom. Each of these plays a critical role in connecting us with God and fosters a spiritual depth that our digital world easily disrupts. What our machines were meant to do in productivity and entertainment has also, as an unintended casualty, taken away the ability to pay sustained attention. Douglas Steere, the quaker teacher, writes that prayer consists of attentiveness, and sin is "anything that destroys this attention."[89] Even the word "attention" is closely related to the French word *attendre*, which means "to wait."[90] We know, intuitively, to engage deeply with God, we need to tame our wild thoughts. Learning to develop our attention is, in essence, learning to become available. It is a willingness to listen to God's voice and obey His calling on our lives. Join me as we, along with Lewis, learn how to daily develop the ability to tame our thoughts and the thousand "wild animals" clamoring for attention.

Three Types of Attention

While many of us tend to think of attention solely in terms of focused concentration, there are actually multiple forms of attention that play significant roles in our daily lives. Understanding these different types of attention is crucial, as each serves a unique purpose and contributes to our overall mental and spiritual well-being.

Focused attention is typically what most people think of when discussing this topic. This type of attention is a valuable resource that has limits and needs to be replenished on a regular basis. *Rote attention*, like the kind we use playing a simple video game, washing dishes, knitting, or even taking a coffee break, serves a valuable purpose as a means to refuel the resources needed in focused attention. Even *boredom*, as we will see below, is valuable. A balanced approach to attention involves recognizing the value of boredom, focused attention, and rote attention; incorporating each into our lives in a healthy way.

Boredom

Boredom is defined as an unpleasant emotional state in which the individual feels a pervasive lack of interest and difficulty concentrating on the current activity.[91] Psychologically, boredom is a signal that our current situation is not fulfilling our need for engagement and stimulation. In today's rapidly moving, technology-focused society, boredom is often viewed as something to be avoided at all costs. With technology offering limitless distractions—from social media to streaming services—every possible free moment of our day can be filled. Although these distractions can temporarily relieve boredom, they may also prevent us from participating in more meaningful activities that require deeper reflection and effort. Despite its negative reputation, boredom has several positive aspects that can act as a powerful catalyst for change and personal development.

Catalyst for Creativity

Boredom can be the birthplace for creativity. When our minds are not focused on specific tasks, our thoughts wander and develop connections in other areas of life, leading to a creative state of mind. Many great works of art, literature, and scientific discoveries have been born out of periods of boredom. The renowned physicist Richard Feynman developed some of his most innovative ideas while doodling and during bouts of boredom.[92] Winner of the Nobel Prize in Physics in 1965 for his work in quantum electrodynamics, which laid the groundwork for much of modern theoretical physics, Feynman described how boredom leads to innovation in three ways: First, in daydreaming, Feynman found that as his mind wandered, new ideas and insights appeared. The relaxation of mind or openness to unstructured thought was for Feynman the process of creative problem-solving. Second, Feynman was dedicated to curiosity-driven exploration as he pursued very strange interests, purely for their own sake—safe-cracking or playing the bongo drums. These odd and diverse interests in no small measure enriched his life and also gave him some insights to bring back to his work on physics. Finally, Feynman valued unstructured time where he wasn't working on anything in particular that had to come out some way. It was this time that allowed him to make those weird connections between things and reflect at a deep level.

Trigger for Self-Reflection

Boredom provides an opportunity for introspection and daydreaming. When we are not distracted by external stimuli, we can turn our attention inward and reflect on our goals, values, and desires. This self-reflection can lead to greater self-awareness and to spiritual and personal growth. Think of daydreaming as an internal superpower. In all other forms of cognition, we experience and understand our world from the outside in. Daydreaming allows us to understand the world from the inside out, tapping into who we are, our interactions, memories, and future possibilities.

We can learn a lot from those who have dedicated their lives to the boredom superpower. Albert Einstein, one of the greatest thinkers of all time, was a big believer in deep reflection, saying, "It's not that I'm so smart, it's just that I stay with the problems longer."[93] Mother Teresa valued the silence that can accompany boredom. She believed that it is only in those silent moments in life, far from clamor and commotion, that a person can really meet God and find His love and peace. She speaks of how silence becomes a condition for prayer and spiritual growth, saying, "In the silence of the heart, God speaks."[94]

Prompt for New Interests

Boredom often drives us to seek out new activities and interests. It can push us out of our comfort zones and encourage us to explore new hobbies, skills, and experiences. Many people have discovered new passions, such as learning a musical instrument or picking up a new sport, as a result of feeling bored and seeking something new to engage their minds. Boredom can be the "check engine" light in our lives that warns us we are not doing what we want to be doing and pushes us to take a new direction. As Christians, the periods of solitude and stillness we often find ourselves in when we're bored are critical as we learn to be still (Psalm 46:10) and wait on hearing from God (Isaiah 40:31).

Focused Attention

One of the most significant books ever written on developing focused attention is Arnold Bennett's classic book, *How to Live on 24 Hours a Day*.[95] Even more significant is that it was first published in 1908, well before the internet and today's modern distractions. Bennet's book, however, provides timeless wisdom on the art of managing one's time and mental focus. His insights are particularly relevant in the context of cultivating a focused and attentive life, especially when it comes to prayer. His ideas have transformed my inner thought life in terms of the importance of controlling what goes on in the brain, the process of maintaining persistent focus, the ability to focus our thoughts at any time, and the significance of a reflective mood. Developing our attention, even in the midst of endless distractions, is possible. It takes practice. But Bennett emphasizes several key principles that, with discipline, will help us clear our vision and avoid things that dull our vision.

Taking the Brain Captive

First, we need to recognize the supreme importance of realizing that nothing happens to us outside our own brains. Nothing can hurt us or give us pleasure except that the brain processes it. It is, therefore, crucial to master the art of controlling our mental activities—focusing attention on what truly matters rather than being at the mercy of external distractions. The apostle Paul calls us to tame our brain in this way, encouraging us to "take captive every thought to make it obedient to Christ" (2 Corinthians 10:5). By taking our thoughts captive, we can align our minds with God's will and purpose, developing a deeper relationship with Him.

Hold a Meeting with Yourself

Second, Bennett describes a process that has proven very powerful for me in developing a focused thought life. The process involves setting aside a dedicated time to meet with yourself on a topic until it is thoroughly understood. Bennett likens this practice to physical exercise: Just as muscles grow stronger with regular training, our ability to concentrate improves with consistent effort.

I have used the time in my morning run or walk to practice this technique. I think we have all experienced the clarity that comes with spending time in nature. As it turns out, research supports this experience. Our brains, according to attention restoration therapy (ART), become clearer and sharper while in nature. Researchers noticed that people who spent time in a quiet rural setting, close to nature, exhibited greater attentiveness, stronger memory, and generally improved cognition. The researchers concluded that even brief interactions with nature can produce significant increases in our ability to control our thoughts.[96]

Here is how it works. I suggest you go on a walk or easy run. Before you leave, decide on a specific topic for your focused attention. I have often focused on a personal or family problem or a work problem. Next, set a timer for ten minutes to focus your thoughts on this topic alone. When you notice your mind wander to another topic you must bring your mind back to the subject. This focused time on that topic should also generally involve prayer. Use the time to focus your prayer time on the specific topic and shift into and out of prayer and cognitive focus on the topic. For an even deeper dive into focused attention, I advise a quarterly overnight retreat. I have personally gained enormous insight from these special times of solitude and focus. To ensure the time is productive, take time to plan details for how you will minimize distractions and how you will designate times for your focused prayer sessions. Be sure you take the time to reflect on what is important, journal on your life's top priorities, and develop clarity for what truly matters.

While I think this technique works best in nature, you can practice the technique anywhere you have time alone with your thoughts—on a commute, in the shower, or washing the dishes. As you practice this technique more, you will find that your skill of focusing thought improves such that you will be able to gain insights at any time, regardless of external circumstances. Applying this to your spiritual life, you can use everyday moments to connect with God through prayer and reflection. Whether you are waiting in line, traveling, or performing routine tasks, these moments can become opportunities to focus your thoughts on God's presence and guidance.

Build the Habit, Reap the Reward

Taking the time for building focused prayer sessions into our life is a critical component of a well-lived life. It is only through this reflective thinking that we can develop deeper meaning and understand the implications of our experiences, actions, and beliefs. The only way this happens, however, is by setting aside time to ponder life's fundamental questions and our relationship with God. In essence, we are investing our time in what truly matters. Through regular reflection, we can reassess our priorities and align our daily activities with our core values and goals. The psalmist writes, "I will consider all your works and meditate on all your mighty deeds" (Psalm 77:12). By regularly engaging in reflective prayer and meditation, we can gain greater insight into God's will and purpose for our lives.

Rote Attention

Rote attention, generally downplayed as performing mindless or unproductive tasks, actually plays a very important role in spiritual life. This kind of attention, which requires us to do things over and over in a routine fashion, gives the mind rest and recuperation. In *Attention Span*, Gloria Mark describes the experience of the renowned poet Maya Angelou to explain the importance of this type of attention.[97] Angelou, it seems, knew the importance of a balanced view of attention, describing her brain as "Big Mind" and "Little Mind." Big Mind is the state of deep focus and creative thinking in which she would engage in deep thoughts about her poetry and larger ideas. It is in this state that substantial creation and innovation took place. Angelou told of how she used to isolate herself from the bustle of everyday life to access her Big Mind through working in a hotel room so nothing could disturb her. Little Mind, on the other hand, refers to the ordinary, everyday thoughts that preoccupy our mind as we do routine tasks. Angelou balanced intense periods of focus with playing games that required little attention. Rote attention gives our focused minds, when stretched to the limit, a chance to repair and rebuild, just as the body does with sleep.

Take the simple task of washing dishes. This is a rather mundane chore, and there is very little by way of cognitive demand that this could make on our minds. This is precisely where most people are occupied with thoughts about their day, ruminating about life's problems, or praying. The rhythm produced by repetition can be meditative, opening up a space for us to hear God. This is certainly not a new idea. Monks and nuns have for centuries applied the use of repetitive activities, such as chanting, walking, or bead counting to enhance their experience of spiritual life.

Science has gone further to prove the need for rote attention. Mark's research has shown that doing highly routine tasks dramatically reduces stress and enhances mental health. Her research shows that such activities may put the brain in a sort of passive mode, giving it a chance to recover from the stress of concentrating.[98] A report by the Association for Psychological Science discovered that individuals who engage in everyday, repetitive activities exhibit enhanced creativity and problem-solving skills.[99] Such activities, provide a kind of a mental break, allowing the subconscious mind to process information and come up with new insights. For Christians, this equates to providing the space to hear from and experience a closer relationship with God.

A Balanced View of Social Media

Given this perspective, social media and performing mindless tasks like playing Candy Crush actually serve a valuable purpose. Despite how much Christians, and people in general, justifiably bemoan the destructive nature of social media, we need a balanced view of this technology that addresses the times we "check out" on our phones. Like most things in life, it is about creating a healthy balance and boundaries for time spent with these technologies. Specifically, Mark's research has shown me the importance of tasks like social media and video games that promote rote attention in several areas:

- ❖ ***Cognitive breaks.*** When we do things like scrolling through social media or playing a not-so-complicated game, our brains are provided with a break from tough, cognitive tasks. These breaks are necessary if we want to stay mentally energetic and focused for longer periods.

❖ *Mental reset.* This helps to clean out mental clutter and reduce cognitive load. When we are disengaged from focused attention, our brain is allowed to regroup, and we are often more productive and creative when we go back to the task at hand.

❖ *Stress reduction.* Engaging in fun and interesting activities that are also silly reduces stress and puts people in a better mood. Being in this type of positive emotional state might contribute to better overall cognitive functioning and mental health.

❖ *Replenishing attention resources.* The attention that one can give to any specific matter is limited. Attention gets exhausted with prolonged concentration in a demanding job. Doing simple and enjoyable activities can replenish the resources of attention providing new opportunities to gain concentration and perform well.

❖ *Balancing work and play.* Mark believes we should balance heavy-duty, deep-concentration work with relaxation and play. This balance helps prevent one from burning out and at the same time keeps them productive.

Including rote attention in our spiritual lives is not a matter of doing yet another thing, squeezing it in our already full days; instead, it is actually stopping to note and value what exists amidst the restful, contemplative times we all have. It is through acknowledging the spiritual importance of everyday activities that we can use these daily activities as chances to grow spiritually.

Developing a Focused Prayer and Thought Life

We can cultivate a more focused and intentional approach to our spiritual practice. Here are some practical steps to apply these insights to developing a focused prayer life:

❖ *Quiet time.* Develop a quiet time daily in which you are alone, free of distractions, and in which you deliberately focus your heart and your thoughts upon God. I have a habit of starting every morning with prayer and reading God's Word. Personally, I have found the first thing in the morning tends to work the best as it eliminates the rest of life that is ready to encroach on this sacred time.

❖ *Prayer walks and personal retreats.* Dedicate an hour each day to focused meditation on a particular scripture verse or aspect of God's character. Make sure to practice this focused concentration regularly as you train your ability to center attention in prayer.

❖ *Personal retreats.* Set aside one-to-two days every three months to reflect about your life situation and realign your focus on God. Use the time to consider ways by which God has worked in your life, lessons you have learned, where further growth is needed, and use a journal to capture your thoughts and prayers and document your times of reflective thinking.

❖ *Redeem idle moments.* During the day, redeem moments of waiting or routine work by brief prayer or reflection on these moments. Such routine can help you remain in touch with God and cultivate a prayerful attitude. Remember that you can focus your thoughts at any time or in any place.

❖ *Adopt "focused" technology.* We have all fallen for the meager profits promised by the latest app or service and have failed to count the cost in terms of our most precious resource—time, the minutes of our life. While technology can quite easily distract us, break our attention, and disrupt the flow of our activities, it can also be harnessed to encourage and enable our efforts in focus and reflection—spending our lives on things of ultimate importance. Here are a few ideas that have worked well for me: (1) Use tools that can reduce distractions, such as the time management applications, focus timers, or software that helps in blocking distractions. (2) Listen to audiobooks or sermons during monotonous tasks. (3) Use noise-canceling headphones, playing focused music such as classical or instrumental worship. (4) Turn off social media and text notifications.

❖ **Make room for God in your daily routines.** Do things like driving, gardening, cleaning the house—or any other rote task that you do—not surrounded by digital noise to give time for mental rest, reflection, and the opportunity for you to hear the still small voice of God.

God is calling you to the attentive life amidst the distractions of the digital age. Embrace boredom, focused, and rote attention while you become intentional with your digital tools. This can lead to a more focused and fulfilling life of honoring God with your mind and fostering deeper connections with yourself and others. As you navigate the challenges of modern technology, may you continually seek to "be still and know" the presence and guidance of God in your life.

Application Guide

For a detailed checklist to evaluate and reduce your digital habits, download the Application Guide here[1]. You'll find practical steps to begin reclaiming your focus today.

Key Points

❖ Prayer requires focused attention, which is increasingly challenged by digital distractions.

❖ Strengthen your prayer life by cultivating focused attention, free from digital distractions.

❖ Embrace the value of rote attention and boredom as tools for deepening your spiritual connection.

❖ Practice methods like prayer walks and meetings with yourself to enhance your ability to focus during prayer.

Questions for Reflection

1. Read Psalm 46:10. How does this verse speak to the need for focused attention in your prayer life? What steps can you take to "be still" in a noisy world?

2. What role does rote attention play in your spiritual practices? How can you incorporate this type of attention more intentionally?

3. Consider the challenges of maintaining focus in prayer. What strategies have you found effective, and what new approaches might you try?

---

1. https://www.thefocusedfaith.com/free

The Lost Art of Deep Reading: Navigating the Noise to Find Truth

Your word is a lamp for my feet, a light on my path.

–Psalm 119:105

Christians feed on Scripture. . . we assimilate it, take it into our lives in such a way that it gets metabolized into acts of love, cups of cold water, missions into all the world, healing and evangelism and justice in Jesus' name.

–Eugene Peterson

I love to run. One individual who has inspired me in this area is Dean Karnazes. He is among a small—and a bit crazy—group of ultra marathon runners. These are individuals who run at least fifty miles at a time in the worst possible conditions—for fun. Mr. Karnazes has gone well beyond even this amazing feat, doing things like running fifty miles in fifty states in fifty days at the age of forty-four![100] Today Karnazes is the recipient of the President's Council on Sports, Fitness and Nutrition Lifetime Achievement Award and one of *Time* Magazine's "100 Most Influential People in the World."

His books have inspired millions, including me, to run. And critically, they've brought awareness to this simple fact: *There is a correct and incorrect way to run.* For me this was a bit of revelation because I believed, incorrectly, that running was something we all knew, intuitively, how to do. The goal of training, in my simple way of thinking, was to simply increase total miles over time. Karnazes explains how, at the beginning of his own research into running, he was consistently plagued with injuries in training for long runs. Like me, he was plagued by shin splints and stress fractures that would consistently stop him from reaching his goals. Yet in his research he learned how the Tarahumara, a Native American tribe, were able to run ultra long distances, barefoot, and without injury! By studying this tribe, he noticed the key to their unbelievable abilities: They had had a biomechanically efficient style that minimizes injury, and maximized endurance. Karnazes incorporated these insights into his training regimen, learning to run with a midfoot strike and maintaining a more natural gait.

His exploration led him, and eventually me, to adapt this running style to enhance efficiency, reduce injury, and deepen the connection to the natural act of running. I quickly learned that I run very differently when using minimalist shoes. The lessons I learned running in minimalist shoes translated into a new way of running that has kept me relatively injury free and has recaptured my joy of the run.

The reason I share this story is that like running, reading is a skill that most of us—incorrectly—believe we have been trained to do at a young age. The reality is, in a world filled with digital distractions, most of us are reading wrongly, and we need to relearn how to read. *Deep reading requires intentional adjustments and disciplined practice* to regain the focus and comprehension we once had. The loss of deep reading in our lives as a culture is having a tremendous effect on us individually and collectively. For example, one of the most fascinating effects I will describe in this chapter is how we are losing an ability to empathize with others. As a Christian, this was an eye opener for me and one of the main reasons I decided to learn to read . . . again.

My Reading Journey

I have always loved to read. Like so many people I have talked with while writing this book, I noticed that around the mid-nineties, the birth of the internet, it was becoming increasingly hard for me to stay engaged with a book. Nicholas Carr, in *The Shallows*, describes my experience perfectly:

> Over the past few years, I've had an uncomfortable sense that someone, or something, has been tinkering with my brain, remapping the neural circuitry, reprogramming the memory. My mind isn't going—so far as I can tell—but it's changing. I'm not thinking the way I used to think. I can feel it most strongly when I'm reading. Immersing myself in a book or a lengthy article used to be easy. My mind would get caught up in the narrative or the turns of the argument, and I'd spend hours strolling through long stretches of prose. That's rarely the case anymore. Now my concentration often starts to drift after two or three pages. I get fidgety, lose the thread, begin looking for something else to do. I feel as if I'm always dragging my wayward brain back to the text. The deep reading that used to come naturally has become a struggle.[101]

Carr's book explained to me perfectly how my previous passion and love for deep reading became so difficult. He goes on to explain the science on how our brains are, literally, being rewired by the digital media that surrounds us to crave the opposite of deep reading: shallow and quick scanning of text. According to Carr's research, when we go online, we enter an environment that promotes both cursory reading and hurried and distracted thinking. Hypertexts, the many links on a site, add to the digital "noise" of reading deeply and frequently because they create rabbit holes of distraction as we click from link to link. While it is technically possible to think deeply while online, just as

THE FOCUSED FAITH

it is possible to think shallowly while reading a book, that is not the type of thinking the technology rewards. Carr explains that our digital world encourages shallow thinking, and our brain plasticity is literally being rewired and is adapting to the demands placed on it. One of Carr's most well-known quotes in his book relates to the long-term influences over how we think: "The Net seizes our attention only to scatter it"[102]

Carr's book, while groundbreaking for its time, was written before the age of social media and our current distractions. Today, the problem is much worse than Carr describes because the algorithms that run the attention economy are designed to keep you scrolling. When we read online, we almost always fail to read with any clear direction because the text we read online is curated by algorithms, compromising our ability to navigate the information we consume. The browsers or news feeds are deliberately designed for inactive reading and to keep us scrolling on.[103]

We Are Reading More . . . and Less

The digital age has definitely translated into reading more words per day but less books.

Here is the startling research on this:

❖ According to The American Time Use Survey, a sample of 26,000 Americans, found that from 2004 to 2017 the percentage of men who read for pleasure had fallen by 40 percent! For women, it had fallen by 29 percent.[104]

❖ An opinion poll by Gallup found that the proportion of Americans who never read a book in any year tripled between 1978 and 2014.[105]

❖ Data from the National Endowment for the Arts' Survey of Public Participation in the Arts indicates a drop in the percentage of American adults who read at least one book in the previous twelve months. From 1992 to 2017, the percentage fell from 61 percent to less than 53 percent.[106]

❖ In 2017, the average American spent seventeen minutes a day reading books and 5.4 hours on their phone.[107]

Johann Hari poignantly summarizes our current state:

> For many of us, reading a book is the deepest form of focus we experience—you dedicate many hours of your life, coolly, calmly, to one topic, and allow it to marinate in your mind. This is the medium through which most of the deepest advances in human thought over the past four hundred years have been figured out and explained. And that experience is now in free fall.[108]

Deep Reading and Our Faith

As I researched and become aware of the broad impact of shallow reading, I grew very interested in learning what effect this was having on me personally—as an academic, in my personal life, and as a Christian. As Christians, I have learned about two critical areas impacted by our devices that cause us to fall into shallow reading: shallow reading of God's Word and a loss of empathy for our brothers and sisters.

Shallow Reading of Scripture

First, let's examine the obvious one: shallow reading of God's Word. Jesus calls us to love Him with our heart, soul, and *mind*. As our

THE FOCUSED FAITH

minds lose the ability to deeply focus on God's Word, we develop a shallow cognitive understanding of God's Word. Deep reading allows us to process the complex ideas found in God's Word and foster the critical thinking skills needed to think all aspects of the text. Regular exposure to the varied language and vocabulary found in Scripture enhances our linguistic abilities. It helps us learn new words in context, understand their nuanced meanings, and incorporate them into our understanding.

Deep reading has a long history with the Christian faith. The practice of meditative reading, or *lectio divina* (Latin for "divine reading"), involves slowly and contemplatively reading of Scripture to seek deeper spiritual understanding.[109] This method aligns with the need for deep reading, as it requires focus, patience, and a quiet environment free from distractions. By engaging deeply with biblical texts, Christians can cultivate a stronger faith and a more intimate relationship with God. This ancient practice consists of four steps: reading (*lectio*), meditation (*meditatio*), prayer (*oratio*), and contemplation (*contemplatio*). It encourages us to slow down and immerse ourselves in the text, allowing the Holy Spirit to illuminate deeper meanings and personal insights.

The key to developing a deeper understanding of a text is to move beyond passive or shallow reading and become an active reader. Have you ever noticed that many of the most respected and godly men and women in your church often have Bibles—physical Bibles, not smartphones—that are the most highlighted and full of notes? The opposite of shallow reading is active reading and is a practice that involves much more than simply reading the text; it actively engages by highlighting or underlining text, writing notes, and comparing other texts.

Commonplace books—that is, a personal journal or notebook used to collect and organize quotes, ideas, observations, and information from various sources for reflection and reference—are a powerful way to become a deeper thinker and active reader. Prevalent since the Renaissance, these books function as a repository for various books, letters, speeches, and other written materials that the reader finds useful and/or meaningful. Alongside the excerpts, the reader writes their own interpretations, reflections, or comments.[110] For many, a journal for devotions, or journaling directly in the Bible, act as a powerful kind of commonplace book. The important thing to remember is that we remember much more of what we read when we interact with the Bible or other books beyond simply reading the text.

Lack of Empathy

The second area impacted by shallow reading may not be as obvious but is critical to our lives as Christians: empathy. Before we look at the research on shallow reading and empathy, let's consider Jesus' life as our example. His life was filled with empathy, demonstrating his deep understanding and compassion for others. He healed the blind man and leper. He wept at the tomb of Lazarus, showing his empathy for the family before raising him from the dead. He fed the 5000 when they were hungry, forgave sins, comforted the grieving, and reached out to the marginalized, like the Samaritan woman at the well, in which he broke social and cultural barriers to offer hope. Most of all, while Jesus suffered for us on the cross, He asked for forgiveness to those who crucified Him, saying, "Father, forgive them for they do not know what they are doing" (Luke 23:34).

Despite the importance of empathy in Jesus' life, contemporary research shows that the world has a dismal view on the importance of empathy. A notable study conducted by the University of Michigan analyzed data from nearly 14,000 college students over thirty years and found that today's college students are about 40 percent less empathetic than those from the 1980s and 1990s.[111] This decline has been particularly steep since the year 2000. The study attributes the decline to increased exposure to media, particularly violent video games and social media, along with cultural shifts toward self-centered thinking and behavior. In another study, the researchers found that the mere presence of a mobile device, even just lying on the table, can lower the empathy between two friends.[112]

The lack of empathy in our world is clearly a complex problem involving many causes and potential solutions. However, one of the most fascinating and life-changing findings for me was learning there is a link between deep reading and empathy. Researchers have found that when we engage deeply with a book—particularly literary fiction—we expose ourselves to the inner lives of characters, understanding their thoughts, emotions, and motivations. This immersive experience enhances our ability to empathize with others in real life.[113] Researchers have found a significant correlation between the amount of time spent reading novels and the ability to read other people's emotions. They summarize the findings saying that reading is far from a meaningless activity that ends when the reader closes the book. It turns out that the act of reading transforms us as it fosters empathy through exposure to diverse perspectives and emotional experiences. As Christians, our single greatest text for deep reading can and should be the Word of God. While I did not find studies to prove the link, I know from personal experience that my love for others, and empathy, grows as I read God's Word and learn from the example of Jesus.

Aside from the spiritual reasons to rekindle our love for deep reading, I think there are compelling personal reasons to develop the skill of deep reading. First, I believe a life filled with deep reading is a good life. Books, in particular the Bible, nourish us in contrast to the messages we receive from social media. Social media tends to feed the flesh in our sinful nature, leaving us eventually drained and unhappy. In contrast, I like the person I become when I am consistently reading deeply. I find the person I become is shaped, like the example of the shovel, by the technologies I use, and I prefer to be shaped by books.

Practical Methods to Develop Deep Reading

Below are some practical ways to incorporate the habit of deep reading into your life:

❖ *Choose the environment.* Find a quiet, comfortable reading space free from digital distractions. Ensure that you use the space for this purpose only so that your mind can wire itself to focus every time it is in that space. This focused setting cues your brain that it's deep reading time, which helps you sustain focus.

❖ *Create a reading routine.* Have set times each day for deep reading. Regularity will train your brain, taking these reading slots seriously helps cue your brain about what to expect and when. The quiet time in the morning is a great way to begin carving out time to read the Word of God. Be sure to seek out other books throughout the day and develop a regular habit that makes it a natural part of your daily routine.

❖ *Use physical books.* For many people, focusing on reading physical books instead of digital versions can be beneficial. I love my Kindle, but for many people, holding a book does wonders for adding focus and reducing the urge to multitask. It's also free of all the notifications and hyperlinks that create distractions common in digital formats. There is also general scientific evidence that people comprehend and retain less of what they take in on screens.[114]

❖ *Meditate on God's Word.* Before reading, take some time to prepare yourself in prayer to clear your mind and enhance focus. For many of us, reading God's Word is the most profound type of meditation we do. As you coolly and calmly read one topic for an extended period, make sure to take time after you have read to allow it to marinate in your mind.

❖ *Become an active reader.* Consider creating a commonplace book as a way to get more deeply engaged with a text. Simply highlighting texts is one of the strongest methods to improve your comprehension when reading deeply. For example, when I was researching this book, I adopted a highlighting system: yellow for information that is important, red for information that is very critical, and blue for personal stories that resonated with me. The best part is that Kindle has a function that will export all of your highlights to one file, allowing you to review the best parts of your book. For printed book lovers, take notes in margins, highlight or underline important points, and write summaries. This will really reinforce the practice of understanding and remembering. When you annotate a text, it lets you process and reflect on what you are reading. It is through slowing down and more carefully taking things in—through annotation, mark-up, and notes as we read—that we deeply understand and intake information.

❖ *Limit multitasking.* Avoid multitasking while reading. Focus solely on the text and resist the urge to check your phone or engage in other activities. Multitasking divides your attention and reduces the quality of your reading experience. Committing to single-tasking enhances your ability to immerse yourself in the material.

❖ *Read aloud.* Reading aloud can slow down your reading pace and improve comprehension. It engages different cognitive processes and helps you to focus on the meaning and nuances of the text. This technique can be particularly useful when reading complex or challenging material.

❖ *Join a reading group.* Participating in a book club or reading group can provide motivation and accountability. Discussing texts with others enhances your understanding and encourages deeper engagement. Group discussions expose you to different perspectives and interpretations, enriching your reading experience.

❖ *Set reading goals.* Establish specific goals for your reading sessions, such as finishing a certain number of chapters or understanding key concepts. Clear objectives provide direction and help maintain focus. Choose physical books over ebooks and print over digital magazine subscriptions. Invest in a good printer and print out online articles you intend to read more deeply. Organize your books and magazines so you can refer to them easily and compile your printed articles in ring binders.

❖ *Change your perspective of reading.* For many, reading has become something we do to fill dead time. Change your perspective to view deep reading as a critical part of your life, and ensure that you have a plan to include deep reading into every day as a conscious decision.

Application Guide

Reclaim your love for deep reading with helpful strategies found in the Application Guide here[1]. Download it at ww.thefocusedfaith.com/free and start cultivating a life of deep, focused study.

Key Points

❖ The digital age has eroded our ability to read deeply, affecting empathy and understanding.

❖ Deep reading is essential for spiritual growth and must be intentionally cultivated.

❖ Reclaim your ability to read deeply by creating intentional habits that resist the superficial nature of digital reading.

❖ Recognize the impact of shallow reading on your empathy and understanding.

❖ Establish a daily or weekly routine dedicated to deep reading, particularly of Scripture.

Questions for Reflection

1. Read Psalm 119:105. How does deep reading of Scripture guide your life, and how has this practice been impacted by digital distractions?

2. What are the benefits of deep reading, particularly of the my , in developing empathy and spiritual insight?

---

1. https://www.thefocusedfaith.com/free

3. Reflect on your current reading habits. How can you create a routine that encourages deep, focused reading in your spiritual life?

Purging Distraction: The Transformative Journey of Detox and Flow

Therefore, since we are surrounded by such a great cloud of witnesses, let us throw off everything that hinders and the sin that so easily entangles.

And let us run with perseverance the race marked out for us.

–Hebrews 12:1

The greatest victory is that which requires no battle.

–Sun Tzu

Though I know there will be no sadness in heaven, I do wonder sometimes if there will be any sense of regret when we one day learn of the opportunities we could have pursued, but instead we blindly followed our distractions. I would like to share with you a profound true story about my great, great grandfather, who succumbed to the distractions of his day. The amazing thing is that it is highly likely your life has been directly touched by my great, great grandad's decisions too.

His name was William H. Bovee, and in 1848 he came to San Francisco. Prior to the move, he came west from New York, where he had a successful business roasting coffee but lost it due to a fire. Upon arriving in San Francisco at age twenty-seven, he found a fourteen-year-old protégé to help him build up his coffee business again. The coffee business became wildly successful as the two became among the very first to offer pre-roasted beans in tins to the thousands

THE FOCUSED FAITH

of men heading to the hills to find gold. In 1850, my great, great grandfather named his company the Pioneer Steam Coffee and Spice Mills. Then in 1859 he made a terrible mistake: He sold the business to his protégé and followed the masses to strike it rich finding gold. He had accumulated a $250,000 fortune in the coffee business, and in the end he lost it all in the hills of the gold country. I did the math on that number, and it equates to losing approximately $8.5 million today's dollars.

The distraction of my great, great grandad's day was that there was a better life to be found in the hills. I wonder if my life would be different today had he been able to remain focused on the abundant life God had given him in the coffee business. Why? His protégé's name was Jim Folger. Yes, Folger's coffee.[115]

The picture below is a 1852 ad from William Bovee's Coffee and Spice Mill.[116]

The Traditional Detox

In my research, the most typical method for attempting to deal with our distraction in the digital world is through a digital detox. The typical detox allocates a period of time, such as twenty-four hours or up to thirty days, to remove yourself from your device or the aspects of your device that result in your becoming distracted. After the detox, you are then allowed to use your phone again but, hopefully, using more discretion as a result of fasting from your device.

The Problem with the Traditional Digital Detox

Like many of us, I have attempted multiple digital detoxes of my own in an effort to develop better focus and attempt to resolve the feeling of being addicted to my device. Though a detox can be valuable, there are several significant limitations I have personally experienced and have found in the research. First, let's look at the research. In a systematic review of major studies employing a digital detox, I found that researchers conclude (a) a detox does result in decreased use of your smartphone usage, which, to me, is to be expected, and (b) the detox results in decreased depression levels. All other findings from the studies employing a digital detox were not conclusive.[117] In short, the research shows we still don't really know the effectiveness of this method largely because the rules in which a detox are performed (i.e., length of the detox, extent of the detox, etc.) are varied. Other than decreased depression levels, there is no evidence that the digital detox, by itself, will result in any long-term positive effects such as reduced distractions, reduced usage of your phone long term, or improved attention.

In the end, the results of these experiments left me feeling bored, irritable, and lonely as I struggled with how to fill the void of time previously filled with whatever was on my phone. While there were short-term gains in reducing my overall screentime, it seemed that I would quickly pick up my old habits again, and in the long term the detox had little effect.

A New Method

For all these reasons, I would like to propose a unique method for the digital detox based on the research and my personal experiences that I believe results in improved focus and a life filled with more satisfaction. The key distinction in this method is that before the digital detox even begins, before you remove the digital distractions from your life, you identify the tasks that will demand your full attention and fill the vacuum of time left that you previously allocated to your device.

There are three steps to ensure you successfully unplug from pointless distractions *and* reallocate that time to tasks that demand your complete focus:

1. Plan the detox.

2. Implement the detox.

3. Reintroduce tech with added friction.

Step 1: Plan the Detox

The first step in a long-term, successful detox is to identify the things in your life that will act as a powerful antidote to the pull of digital devices during the detox period. In chapter 2, we reviewed the importance of reflecting on your life to identify your flow states: the tasks you are passionate about and which require your complete attention. Prayer, solitude, reading, meditation, reading the Scriptures, and seeking counsel from others are all ways God can help reveal multiple flow activities in your life.

To help with this, using a blank sheet of paper, write out your plan on how you will spend your time while not being on your device during the detox.

Here is the list I created for this step when I completed my digital fast:

❖ *I will dedicate three-to-five times per week, for at least two hours per session, for writing a total of 3000 words per week.*

❖ *I will dedicate time in my schedule to ensure I run at least four times per week.*

❖ *I will dedicate 50 percent of the time I used to spend listening to music on a run to prayer.*

❖ *I will dedicate three mornings per week in my schedule to go fishing or spend time solitude in God's creation.*

Notice the two key elements in this statement: a commitment to the task and a specific amount of time.

Once you have completed identifying and planning to engage in your flow tasks, you are ready to move on to the detox. The detox will not only remove unwanted distractions but will also free up more time previously wasted to your device for you to pursue the tasks God has uniquely gifted you to perform. During this time, you will do two things: (1) fast from digital distractions on your devices, and (2) aggressively pursue the flow activities.

Remember, the goal for the digital fast is not to simply remove yourself from distractions. It's also to use the time previously outsourced to your devices to engage fully with your flow activities. This is a time to rediscover the abundant life found in the Christian disciplines and in the tasks that will align with your gifts. The apostle Paul's words are especially relevant for your detox: "You were taught, with regard to your former way of life, to put off your old self, which is being corrupted by its deceitful desires; to be made new in the attitude of your minds; and to put on the new self, created to be like God in true righteousness and holiness." (Ephesians 4:22–24). The detox is a powerful way to put off old habits and put on the new. At the end of this fast, you should have a vision for a long-term plan for your life in which digital technologies *serve you* and not the other way around. You should also have a feeling for the types of technologies that will facilitate accomplishing your flow activities and those that will distract you from achieving meaningful outcomes.

Following are several guidelines to ensure your detox is a success:

Create a Digital Detox Plan

If you are like me, you have attempted a digital detox before and failed. Often the reason for a failed attempt is lack of planning. Planning your detox is critical. In planning your detox consider the following important decisions.

First, how long is the detox? One common reason for failing a detox is being overly aggressive with this decision and planning the detox for a week or even longer. While the ideal detox would be on a seven-day vacation, the reality is it is much more difficult for the majority of us to unplug for that length of time. For this reason, start with committing to a twenty-four hour fast. Once you have experienced the benefits from the twenty-four hour fast, plan to do longer periods of time such as a weekend and eventually a week.

Select the Technologies That Will Be the Focus for the Fast

If we are honest, we all have specific digital technologies we know are adding distraction to our lives. For many individuals, watching YouTube videos, social media, or texting are major distractions. Since I committed many years to stop using social media, my most recent distraction has been checking and reading the news. Therefore, there is no universal rule in what applications to avoid during your fast.

Try this exercise: Start with being honest with yourself and ask yourself the question, what digital activities that I currently do that would, if removed, would most improve my focus? Next, write create two columns with the first column labeled "Distractions." List all of your answers in this column. Label the second column, "Flows." In this column, write the list of activities you identified in chapter 2. The idea is that you are planning, in advance, to reallocate the time you currently use for distractions to activities that are linked to an abundant life. In my case, for example, checking and reading the news is in the first column. Prayer, fishing, and running are in the second column. When I was tempted to check news during the fast, I would take the time to silently pray, go fishing, or go for a run.

Get Accountable and Communicate Your Fast to Others

Plan ahead with your employer and family, letting them know about your digital fast. For example, create a simple and brief out-of-office message on your email letting others know when they can expect a return email. You will also want to inform family members so they can support you during this time, and they can help hold you accountable. It will also help to reset their expectations for not getting instant replies to text messages and emails.

Identify the Resources You Will Need During the Fast

We rely on our smartphones for an endless list of legitimate reasons. Driving directions, making notes, and health tracking are just a few examples. Take the time to think through what resources on your phone you normally need, and then develop a workaround to ensure you don't need to use your phone for these tasks. For example, print driving directions before you begin the fast. The reason for this is to ensure that you leave yourself with no excuses for breaking the fast. It will become increasingly difficult to maintain the fast, and "just a quick look at the phone for driving directions" will almost certainly result in seeing notifications and other distractions that will cause you to break your fast.

Write out Your Complete Plan in the Form of a Commitment to Yourself

Be sure you include all details on how you plan to implement your digital detox plan, including rules for what, how, and when it will take place.

To help with this, consider thinking through the following questions based on what you found in the steps above:

- ❖ How long is the fast?

- ❖ What activities do I want to target/eliminate?

- ❖ How will I reallocate the time I previously spent on these activities?

Notice how this written plan helps you identify the timeframe, activities you want to target for the fast, and how you plan to reallocate the time freed from not using your device. Following this list, write the flow activities that you created in the previous step.

Here is how I developed my plan:

During my thirty day fast I will

- ❖ *Stop reading the news on any digital device.*

- ❖ *Instead of reading news after my morning devotion, I will reallocate twenty additional minutes to prayer. [I don't use social media. Checking the news is my biggest source of distraction].*

❖ *Instead of checking my phone to read the news during the day, when I feel the urge to check news on my cell phone, I will instead pray silently.*

❖ *Instead of reading the news at night, I will reallocate the time to reading God's Word or a book that nourishes my soul.*

❖ *I will dedicate three-to-five times per week, for at least two hours per session, for writing a total of 3000 words per week.*

❖ *I will dedicate time in my schedule to ensure I run for at least four times per week.*

❖ *Of the time I used to spend listening to music on a run, I will dedicate 50 percent to prayer.*

❖ *I will dedicate three mornings per week in my schedule to go fishing or spend solitude time in God's creation.*

After you have completed these steps to prepare for your fast, you have positioned yourself for success during your fast.

Step 2: Implement the Detox

Now that you've carefully planned your digital detox, all that is left is to begin. This is where the real challenge comes.

To ensure that your detox is both effective and life changing, following are several guidelines to follow:

Commit to the Process

First and foremost, commit yourself to using this time to enter into a new way of life, even if just for a short period. I strongly suggest starting each day in prayer and spending time reading Scripture or a devotional that reinforces your commitment to the fast. Take the time to reflect on your reasons for the detox and the benefits of a more focused mind.

Engage Fully in Your Flow Activities

During the detox, immerse yourself in the flow activities you identified in your planning phase. These activities are not just fillers to occupy the vacuum of time left open by fasting from your devices. Your flow activities should engage your mind and spirit in meaningful, life-giving pursuits. Plan to reallocate your impulse to check your phone into one of these activities. For instance, if you planned to dedicate time to prayer, use those moments to dive deeper into conversation with God, seeking His guidance and presence. If reading or writing was on your list, allow yourself to get lost in the words, letting them transport you to a place of focus and creativity.

Remember, the goal is not merely to fill the void left by your phone, but to rediscover the richness of a life lived with intention. The more you engage in these activities, the more you'll find that your desire for digital distractions diminishes. *Ultimately, this is the goal of your detox: to see the possibilities of a life less tethered to screens and more connected to God, the present moment, and those around us.*

Monitor Your Emotions and Prayer Life

As you move through the detox, pay close attention to your emotional state. It is natural to experience discomfort, restlessness, or even frustration as you withdraw from the constant stimulation provided by digital devices. Instead of seeing these emotions as barriers, view them as opportunities for growth. These feelings are signals that your mind and body are adjusting to a new rhythm that isn't dictated by the incessant demands of technology.

During this phase, use the time to deepen your prayer life. When you feel an impulse to check your phone, pause and take a moment to pray silently. I have found that all of these "micro prayers" throughout the day add up to feeling much more connected with our Savior. Prayerfully acknowledge the impulse to check your phone and then consciously choose to redirect your attention to a task that aligns with your flow activities. Over time, these prayerful pauses will become a powerful tool in breaking the habit of mindless scrolling and checking.

Stay Accountable

Accountability is key to the success of your detox. Keep your family, friends, or a trusted mentor informed of your progress. Share with them the struggles you encounter and the victories you experience along the way. Accountability like this will encourage you to reflect on your journey in real-time, reinforcing your commitment to the process.

Consider keeping a journal during the detox to document your thoughts, emotions, and any insights you gain. Writing down your experiences can help solidify your learning and provide a record of how your relationship with technology is evolving. It also serves as a reminder of the progress you've made, especially on days when the detox feels particularly challenging.

Embrace the Discomfort

Finally, embrace the discomfort that comes with stepping away from the digital world. It's in this discomfort that real transformation occurs. Just as a muscle grows stronger when it's pushed to its limits, your ability to focus and live with intention will strengthen as you push through the challenges of the detox. Trust that God is with you in this process, refining and shaping you for greater things.

At the end of each day, take time to reflect on what you've learned about yourself, your habits, and your relationship with technology. Offer these reflections to God in prayer, asking for continued strength and guidance as you move forward.

Always remember that the goal is not to simply break free from distractions. More than that, it is to lay the groundwork for a more focused, intentional, and abundant life.

Step 3: Re-introduce Tech with Added Friction

After you finish the fast, spend at least one day to reflect on and pray about the digital fast. Manoush Zomorodi compares the process to parenting in her book *Bored and Brilliant*:[118]

> Smartphones behave like a four-year-old child. If you let kids run wild, then they learn that it's perfectly okay to do that. But as parents, we can teach our kids better rules. Likewise, we can teach our smartphones better rules. We can turn them from devices that constantly interrupt us into devices that protect our attention. Let's use the word "purposeful." As a society, we have decided—much like our beloved devices—it's either on or off. You know, the parents who don't let their kids have any screen time versus those who believe kids should have unlimited access to Minecraft because it's creative. Distraction doesn't come from devices. It is an internal problem. If the problem is internal, that means no matter how fast technology is moving around us, the solution lies inside us.

THE FOCUSED FAITH

Author Cal Newport reminds us that adopting the Amish mindset towards technology can be a valuable asset at this stage.[119] The Amish community is known for its deliberate approach to technology, which emphasizes tools that enhance their way of life without compromising their values. For instance, they may use a hand-cranked washing machine but avoid electric ones to maintain simplicity and independence from the world. They prioritize technologies that promote community, simplicity, and sustainability. In exchange, they reject those that negatively impact their faith, social bonds, or introduce unnecessary complexity. This intentionality in tool selection ensures that the benefits of technology outweigh the potential drawbacks.

Just as the Amish carefully select which technologies to integrate, we can choose apps that genuinely enhance our lives. This involves evaluating whether an app contributes to long-term goals and well-being rather than providing fleeting satisfaction. Newport has labeled this perspective as a philosophy of life called "Digital Minimalism."[120] This philosophy provides a valuable framework for determining how to reintroduce a digital technology back into your life. It consists of three tests. The technology must first serve something you *deeply value*. Like the Amish mindset, simply offering some benefit is not enough. Second, it must be the *best way to use technology* to serve this value. Third, its role in your life must be bound by a *standard operating procedure* that specifies when and how you use it.

To Reintroduce Tech and Add Friction, Complete the Following Exercise

❖ Create a list of the changes you believe God is calling you to make to your digital lifestyle moving forward. One of the most significant decisions you want to make during this timeframe is what and how you will use digital products moving forward.

❖ Review the list of changes you identified in step one and "add friction" to whatever apps on your smartphone you wish to limit future use.

"Adding friction" to your digital world is an extremely practical way to move forward with the decisions on how or what technologies will be used in your life. Friction refers to the deliberate introduction of obstacles or barriers that make it more difficult to engage in unwanted behaviors on smartphones or devices. This concept leverages the human tendency to seek the path of least resistance. By increasing the effort required to perform certain actions, it becomes easier to avoid those actions altogether. Friction is actually a psychological and behavioral strategy used to reduce or eliminate habitual and impulsive actions.[121] When applied to the digital detox, it means creating an environment where accessing distracting apps or websites requires more steps or effort, thereby discouraging their use. The goal is to disrupt the automatic nature of device usage and encourage more mindful engagement with technology.

Multiple Techniques You Can Use to Add Friction within Your Smartphone

Remove the App. Delete the app completely. Deleting social media apps, for example, is a great way to add friction because it will remove the temptation completely, along with notifications that would draw you into the application. Many people adopt a middle ground by deleting the app completely from the phone and allow themselves a small amount of time via a personal computer or laptop.

Reorganize App Layouts. Move frequently used but non-essential apps (like social media) to the last screen or into folders. This additional step can deter immediate, mindless access.

Disable Notifications. Turn off non-essential notifications to reduce the urge to check your phone. Notifications often act as triggers for distraction. I have personally benefited from iPhone's "focus" feature, which completely eliminates unwanted distractions and notifications.

Use App Blockers. Install applications that block or limit access to certain apps or websites. These tools create digital barriers that require conscious effort to bypass. Apps such as Freedom and Moment are all excellent tools that can add extra friction.

Grayscale Display. Switch your phone's display to grayscale. Research shows lack of color reduces the visual appeal of apps, making them less engaging.[122]

Set Screen Time Limits. Use built-in screen time management tools to set daily limits on app usage. Once the limit is reached, accessing the app requires additional steps.

Store your phone in another room while working or sleeping. The physical distance acts as a significant deterrent to impulsive checking. Alternatively, consider not carrying your phone while at home. Simply plugging the phone in and allowing yourself to check it at healthy intervals is a good way to add friction and reduce distractions.

The bottom line is the more difficult you make it to engage in unwanted behaviors, the better.

Reintroduce digital applications. Review your list from step 1, and develop new ground rules for how or when the technologies can be used.

To do this, you might want to think through your entire day and determine a new normal, for you want to interact with your digital world. Mornings are especially critical and are a good place to begin. For instance, I used to look at my phone the moment I woke up, which would result in reading texts, emails, and notifications that would often generate anxiety or, at minimum, a distracted start to my day. One of the best rules I put in place for myself was to not look at my phone until after I have spent time reading God's Word and prayed for the day. I also do not allow myself to review work email until much later in the morning. I recommend that you create a morning routine that works for you. It will help you start your day focused on God and activities leading to your abundant life. Over the long term, a simple morning routine can make a massive difference in your life.

Write out your complete plan in the form of a commitment to yourself. Be sure you include all details on the specific changes you want to make moving forward and the specific ways you will add friction to make these changes happen. Note you are identifying the activities that you want to delete, continue, or limit with specific parameters for how or when they will be used.

Here are some examples of rules that others have put in place. They may help you think of your own:

❖ I will limit social media to a total time of fifteen minutes during lunch hour on my computer.

❖ I will stop surfing YouTube videos and limit use of YouTube to specific searches.

❖ I will start leaving my phone plugged in and charging while at home.

❖ I will stop carrying my phone with me while at home.

THE FOCUSED FAITH

❖ I will limit the time to text messages on my phone at home to fifteen minutes per day.

❖ I will limit use of video games to two times per week.

❖ I will stop taking out my phone during conversations with others.

❖ I will start focusing on being more present in my conversations.

In my case, after completing my fast, I learned that reading news to fill any downtime in my day is a waste of my time that I wanted to allocate to other areas, including prayer.

Therefore, I developed the following commitments to myself:

❖ *I will continue to leave social media apps off my phone.*

❖ *I will limit the use of social media to a maximum of one hour per week on my laptop [since social media will be needed for promoting this book].*

❖ *I will limit myself to reading the news in long form articles once per week for no more than one hour per week.*

Finally, I want to encourage you to avoid viewing the digital detox as a one-time exercise to abstain from your distractions. *It should be included as an ongoing, regular part of your life.* Do it whenever you start to feel the need to reclaim the abundant life that often gets buried under the weight of distractions. The lesson from my great-great-grandfather William H. Bovee's life illustrates that distractions—whether they come in the form of a gold rush or the incessant ping of a smartphone—can lead us away from the paths that bring true fulfillment. The key lies not only in removing the distractions but also in replacing them with the life-giving activities that align with our God-given purpose.

By planning, implementing, and reintroducing technology with intentionality, we can cultivate a life that is focused and deeply satisfying. This process requires more than just a temporary detox. It requires a reorientation of our priorities and habits in order to allow us to engage fully in the moments that matter most. As we move forward, let us remember that the abundant life is not found in the fleeting pleasures of digital devices but in the richness of a life lived with purpose and presence, deeply rooted in the tasks and relationships that God has placed before us.

Application Guide

For a step-by-step guide on how to perform a digital detox and reduce distractions, download the Application Guide by visiting here[1]. You'll also find tools to help you re-engage with meaningful activities.

Key Points

❖ A digital detox is more than just abstinence; it's about replacing distractions with life-giving activities.

❖ Plan and undertake a digital detox, not just as a form of abstinence but also as a way to replace distractions with meaningful, life-giving activities.

---

1. https://www.thefocusedfaith.com/free

❖ Create a strategy for reintroducing technology with added friction to maintain focus on your goals.

❖ Commit to integrating flow states into your daily life, choosing activities that align with your spiritual and personal growth.

Questions for Reflection

1. Read Hebrews 12:1. How can you "throw off everything that hinders" in the context of digital distractions? What specific steps will you take to pursue this?

2. Have you ever attempted a digital detox? What were the results, and how can you approach it differently to achieve lasting transformation?

3. Discuss the concept of "flow." How can engaging in flow activities help you stay focused and spiritually grounded in a digital world?

Conclusion

❖

Well, we have come to the end of this journey together. At the beginning of this book, we imagined a journey without a map, aimlessly wandering through unfamiliar streets. Through each chapter, we've explored how the attention economy pulls us away from our spiritual path, fragmenting our focus and stealing our joy. But we have also discovered the tools we need to regain control: prayer, solitude, and deep reading. As we close this journey, I invite you to continue pressing on, just as Paul encouraged. Lay down the distractions, pick up the tools you've learned here, and pursue the abundant life that God has prepared for you. Your map is now clear—the destination, more fulfilling than you ever imagined. As you think about developing a new relationship with digital tools to get to your destination, I want to share a quote from Reinke's interview with pastor, theologian, and author John Piper. Here is Piper's response when Reinke asked him about his relationship with technology:

> "I could almost come to tears over how precious they are to me." Yes, they are glowing tools made mostly by men and women who are not submitted to God, he reiterated, and they are tools that open up his life to a thousand convenient temptations, but used with care and discipline, the digital tools are, he said, "a treasure chest of the glories of God."[123]

Indeed, the technologies God has gifted us with are "a treasure chest of the glories of God." Though I have spent the majority of this book warning you about the pitfalls of technology, make no mistake, I share Piper's strong love and emotion for these tools. I count myself among the most fortunate people in the world to have been able to work, study, and teach about these amazing tools for decades.

That said, I sincerely hope you too will grow to love these tools as a treasure chest of the glories of God but recognize their shaping influence on our attention. To that end, here is my prayer for you:

My Prayer for You

I pray you will embark on a journey that continues to explore these wonderful technologies. I pray you will continue to explore the ways in which the attention economy has subtly yet powerfully influenced our lives, fragmented our focus, and can pull us from the abundant life that Jesus promises. I pray you will see that your digital device, while offering convenience and connection, has introduced new challenges that threaten your ability to live a deeply connected, meaningful life.

I pray you will continue to examine the systemic forces at play, including how big tech companies have designed their platforms to capture and hold our attention, often at the expense of our mental, emotional, and spiritual well-being. I pray you will continue to study the physiological and psychological impacts of constant connectivity, including dopamine-driven feedback loops and the pervasive sense of dissatisfaction that we can experience in our daily lives.

I pray that you will embrace the antidote to this pervasive distraction: the abundant life that Jesus calls us to. I pray that you will come to treasure the power of solitude, prayer, deep reading, and the pursuit of flow states—activities that demand our full attention and align with our God-given purpose. I pray you will develop a biblical worldview of technology, recognizing that while technology can be a useful tool, it must not be allowed to shape our lives in ways that are contrary to our values.

Moving forward in your life, I pray you would be intentional in how you engage with your digital world, making deliberate choices that reflect your commitment to living a life that is focused on what truly matters. To do this, I pray would you take practical steps to disconnect from the distractions that dominate our screens and reconnect with the disciplines that deepen our faith and enrich our lives.

I pray you would take what you've learned and apply it to your own life, identifying the areas where you've been distracted and committing to making changes that will help you reclaim your focus. I pray you would plan your own digital detox, not as a one-time event, but as the beginning of a new way of living that prioritizes the abundant life over the fleeting satisfaction of digital distractions.

I pray you too would come to know that the abundant life is not found in the endless scroll of social media or the instant gratification of a notification. It is found in the deep, meaningful connections we build with God, with our loved ones, and with the world around us. It is found in the quiet moments of prayer, in the joy of uninterrupted reading, and in the satisfaction of pursuing our passions with full attention.

I pray you would put down your phone more often, look up, and embrace the life that God has called you to live: a life of purpose, of presence, of peace; a life that resists the pull of the digital world and finds its true joy in the richness of God's love and the beauty of His creation. I pray you would commit that the journey doesn't end here, it begins from there.

Amen.

Preface

[1] Min Kwon, et al., "The Smartphone Addiction Scale: Development and Validation of a Short Version for Adolescents," *PLOS ONE* 8, no. 12 (December 31, 2013): e83558, https://doi.org/10.1371/journal.pone.0083558.

Chapter 1

[2] Michael H. Goldhaber, "The Attention Economy and the Net," *First Monday*, April 7, 1997, https://doi.org/10.5210/fm.v2i4.519.

[3] Tim Wu, *The Attention Merchants: The Epic Scramble to Get Inside Our Heads* (New York: Knopf, 2016).

[4] "Alphabet Revenue 2001–2024," Stock Analysis, accessed July 9, 2024, https://stockanalysis.com/stocks/goog/revenue/.

[5] Tim Hinchliffe, "Big Tech's Addictive Business Model Makes Us 'Attention Vampires,' Distracts From Urgent Threats Like China: 'Social Dilemma' Star Testifies," *The Sociable* (blog), April 27, 2021, https://sociable.co/big-tech/big-tech-addictive-business-model-makes-attention-vampires-distracts-urgent-threats-china-social-dilemma-star-testifies/.

[6] Movie & TV reviews for parents, "Constant Companion: A Week in the Life of a Young Person's Smartphone Use," Common Sense Media, accessed August 6, 2024, https://writcommonsensemedia.org/research/constant-companion-a-week-in-the-life-of-a-young-persons-smartphone-use.

[7] Monica Anderson and Jingjing Jiang, "Teens, Social Media and Technology 2018," *Pew Research Center* (blog), May 31, 2018, https://www.pewresearch.org/internet/2018/05/31/teens-social-media-technology-2018/.

[8] Gloria Mark, *Multitasking in the Digital Age* (Springer Nature, 2022).

[9] "A Day Without Media," A Day Without Media, accessed August 5, 2024, https://withoutmedia.wordpress.com/.

[10] "Study Finds Lure of Entertainment, Work Hard for People to Resist," University of Chicago News, January 27, 2012, https://news.uchicago.edu/story/study-finds-lure-entertainment-work-hard-people-resist.

[11] Alex Kerai, "Cell Phone Usage Statistics: Mornings Are for Notifications," Reviews.org, July 21, 2023, https://www.reviews.org/mobile/cell-phone-addiction/.

[12] Thibaut Meurisse, *Dopamine Detox: A Short Guide to Remove Distractions and Get Your Brain to Do Hard Things* (self-published, 2021).

[13] Susan Greenfield, *Mind Change: How Digital Technologies Are Leaving Their Mark on Our Brains* (Random House, 2015).

[14] Mark, *Multitasking in the Digital Age*.

[15] Mark, *Multitasking in the Digital Age*.

[16] "Industry Ethicist: Social Media Companies Amplifying Americans' Anger for Profit," CBS News, November 6, 2022,

https://www.cbsnews.com/news/tristan-harris-social-media-political-polarization-60-minutes-2022-11-06/.

[17] "Presentable #19: Design Ethics and the Race to the Bottom of the Brain Stem," Relay FM, accessed August 5, 2024, https://www.relay.fm/presentable/19.

[18] "AlgoTransparency," AlgoTransparency, accessed August 5, 2024, https://algotransparency.org/.

[19] Cornelia Sindermann, et al., "Age, Gender, Personality, Ideological Attitudes and Individual Differences in a Person's News Spectrum: How Many and Who Might Be Prone to 'Filter Bubbles' and 'Echo Chambers' Online?" *Heliyon* 6, no. 1 (January 1, 2020), https://doi.org/10.1016/j.heliyon.2020.e03214.

[20] B. J. Fogg, "A Behavior Model for Persuasive Design," in *Proceedings of the 4th International Conference on Persuasive Technology*, Persuasive '09 (New York, NY, USA: Association for Computing Machinery, 2009), 1–7, https://doi.org/10.1145/1541948.1541999.

[21] Bianca Bosker, "What Will Break People's Addictions to Their Phones?" *The Atlantic*, October 8, 2016, https://www.theatlantic.com/magazine/archive/2016/11/the-binge-breaker/501122/.

[22] Dar Meshi, Carmen Morawetz, and Hauke R Heekeren, "Nucleus Accumbens Response to Gains in Reputation for the Self Relative to Gains for Others Predicts Social Media Use," *Frontiers in Human Neuroscience*, 7 (2013): 57063.

[23] Lauren E Sherman, et al., "What the Brain 'Likes': Neural Correlates of Providing Feedback on Social Media," *Social Cognitive and Affective Neuroscience*, 13, no. 7 (2018): 699–707.

[24] Jean M. Twenge and W. Keith Campbell, "Associations between Screen Time and Lower Psychological Well-Being among Children and Adolescents: Evidence from a Population-Based Study," *Preventive Medicine Reports*, 12 (2018): 271–83.

[25] Melissa G Hunt, et al., "No More FOMO: Limiting Social Media Decreases Loneliness and Depression," *Journal of Social and Clinical Psychology*, 37, no. 10 (2018): 751–68.

[26] Cited in Johann Hari, *Stolen Focus: Why You Can't Pay Attention—and How to Think Deeply Again* (Crown, 2023), Kindle.

[27] Fogg, "A Behavior Model for Persuasive Design."

[28] Megha Sharma, "The TikTok Algorithm Explained + Tips to Go Viral," SocialPilot, April 23, 2024, https://www.socialpilot.co/blog/tiktok-algorithm.

[29] "Sean Parker Slams Facebook for 'Exploiting a Vulnerability in Human Psychology,'" TheWrap, accessed August 5, 2024, https://www.thewrap.com/sean-parker-facebook-exploiting-vulnerability-human-psychology/.

Steve Kovach, "Former Facebook Exec Feels 'Tremendous Guilt' for What He Helped Make," Business Insider, accessed August 5, 2024, https://www.businessinsider.com/former-facebook-exec-chamath-palihapitiya-social-media-damaging-society-2017-12.

[30] "Why Tech Leaders Don't Let Their Kids Use Tech," Kidzu, November 13, 2017, https://kidzu.co/health-wellbeing/why-tech-leaders-dont-let-their-kids-use-tech/.

[31] Kovach, "Former Facebook Exec Feels 'tremendous Guilt' for What He Helped Make."

[32] "Bill Gates & Steve Jobs Limited Screen Time for Their Kids," CRM.org, March 15, 2018, https://crm.org/articles/bill-gates-kids-and-steve-jobs-limited-screen-time.

[33] "Why Tech Leaders Don't Let Their Kids Use Tech."

[34] PodBean Development, "Self-Control, " Timothy Keller Sermons Podcast by Gospel in Life, accessed August 5, 2024, http://podcast.gospelinlife.com/e/self-control/.

[35] Jay Y. Kim, *Analog Church: Why We Need Real People, Places, and Things in the Digital Age* (InterVarsity Press, 2020).

[36] Michaeleen Doucleff, "The Truth about Teens, Social Media and the Mental Health Crisis," Houston Public Media, April 25, 2023, https://www.houstonpublicmedia.org/npr/2023/04/25/1171773181/the-truth-about-teens-social-media-and-the-mental-health-crisis/.

[37] Kim, *Analog Church*.

Chapter 2

[38] Clive Staples Lewis, *Mere Christianity*, 1952 (Reprint: Zondervan, 2001), chap. 11, Kindle.

[39] Fisher, *Capitalist Realism*.

[40] Nicholas Carr, *The Shallows: What the Internet Is Doing to Our Brains* (WW Norton & Company, 2020).

[41] Cal Newport, *Digital Minimalism: Choosing a Focused Life in a Noisy World* (Penguin, 2019).

[42] Mahatma Gandhi, *Autobiography: The Story of My Experiments with Truth* (Courier Corporation, 1983).

[43] Sebastian Deterding, et al., "From Game Design Elements to Gamefulness: Defining 'Gamification,'" in *Proceedings of the 15th International Academic MindTrek Conference: Envisioning Future Media Environments*, MindTrek '11 (Tampere, Finland: Association for Computing Machinery, 2011), 9–15, https://doi.org/10.1145/2181037.2181040.

[44] Mihaly Csikszentmihalyi, *Flow: The Psychology of Optimal Experience* (Harper & Row, 1990).

[45] Zoltan Buzady, "Flow, Leadership and Serious Games - a Pedagogical Perspective," *World Journal of Science, Technology and Sustainable Development* 14, no. 2/3 (2017): 204–17, https://doi.org/10.1108/WJSTSD-05-2016-0035.

[46] Kim, *Analog Church*.

[47] Dietrich Bonhoeffer, *Letters and Papers from Prison* (SCM Press, 2013).

[48] Bonhoeffer, *Letters and Papers from Prison*.

[49] Arnold Bennett, *How to Live on 24 Hours a Day: With The Human Machine* (Courier Corporation, 2007).

[50] Mihaly Csikszentmihalyi, "Finding Flow," *Psychology Today*, 2007, https://www.semanticscholar.org/paper/Psychology-Today%3A-Finding-flow-Csíkszentmihályi/8fbcff88d66796ec4d98bcb5e3df9b669b05f61f.

[51] Steven Kotler, *The Rise of Superman: Decoding the Science of Ultimate Human Performance* (Houghton Mifflin Harcourt, 2014).

[52] Jane McGonigal, *Reality Is Broken: Why Games Make Us Better and How They Can Change the World* (Penguin, 2011).

[53] Min Kwon, et al., "The Smartphone Addiction Scale: Development and Validation of a Short Version for Adolescents," *PLOS ONE* 8, no. 12 (December 31, 2013): e83558, https://doi.org/10.1371/journal.pone.0083558.

[54] Eyal Ophir, Clifford Nass, and Anthony D Wagner, "Cognitive Control in Media Multitaskers," *Proceedings of the National Academy of Sciences* 106, no. 37 (2009): 15583–87.

[55] Csikszentmihalyi, *Flow*.

Chapter 3

[56] Quoted in A. L. Cohen-Rose and S.B. Christiansen, "The Hitchhiker's Guide to the Galaxy," *Advances in Consciousness* Research, 35 (2002): 55–66.

[57] John Dyer, *From the Garden to the City: The Redeeming and Corrupting Power of Technology* (Kregel Publications, 2011).

[58] Dyer, "*From the Garden to the City: The Place of Technology in the Story of God*: 9780825433122: Amazon.Com: Books," accessed September 23, 2023, https://www.amazon.com/Garden-City-Place-Technology-Story/dp/0825433126/ref=sr_1_1?crid=2QIQFJEQA45XY&keywords=garden+to+the+city&1.

[59] Dyer, *From the Garden to the City: The Redeeming and Corrupting Power of Technology*.

[60] *Digital Liturgies*, 2023, https://www.crossway.org/books/digital-liturgies-tpb/.

[61] Marshall McLuhan, *Understanding Media: The Extensions of Man* (MIT press, 1994).

[62] Carr, *The Shallows*.

[63] Xiaoyue Liu, et al., "Internet Search Alters Intra- and Inter-Regional Synchronization in the Temporal Gyrus," *Frontiers in Psychology* 9 (March 6, 2018), https://doi.org/10.3389/fpsyg.2018.00260.

[64] Louisa Dahmani and Véronique D. Bohbot, "Habitual Use of GPS Negatively Impacts Spatial Memory during Self-Guided Navigation," *Scientific Reports* 10, no. 1 (April 14, 2020): 6310, https://doi.org/10.1038/s41598-020-62877-0.

[65] *Digital Liturgies*.

[66] Tristan Harris, "How a Handful of Tech Companies Control Billions of Minds Every Day," TED Talks, accessed August 5, 2024, https://www.ted.com/talks/tristan_harris_how_a_handful_of_tech_companies_control_billions_of_min transcript.

Chapter 4

[67] "Doing Something Is Better Than Doing Nothing for Most People, Study Shows, " *UVA Today*, July 3, 2014, https://news.virginia.edu/content/doing-something-better-doing-nothing-most-people-study-shows.

[68] John Mark Comer, *The Ruthless Elimination of Hurry: How to Stay Emotionally Healthy and Spiritually Alive in the Chaos of the Modern World* (Random House Publishing Group, 2019).

[69] Anthony Storr, *Solitude: A Return to the Self* (Macmillan, 1988).

[70] "Founders Online: Journal of a Voyage, 1726," University of Virginia Press, accessed August 6, 2024, http://founders.archives.gov/documents/Franklin/01-01-02-0029.

[71] "Abraham Lincoln's Meditation on the Divine Will," accessed August 6, 2024, http://www.abrahamlincolnonline.org/lincoln/speeches/meditat.htm.

[72] David J. Garrow, "Bearing the Cross: Martin Luther King," *Jr., and the Southern Christian*, 1986.

[73] Steve Wozniak with Gina Smith, *iWoz: Computer Geek to Cult Icon: How I invented the personal computer, co-Founded Apple, and had fun doing it.* (W. W. Norton & Company, 2006).

[74] "Bill Gates Spends Two Weeks Alone In the Forest Each Year. Here's Why," Thrive Global, accessed August 6, 2024, https://community.thriveglobal.com/bill-gates-think-week/.

[75] Scott Barry Kaufman and Carolyn Gregoire, "Executives, Protect Your Alone Time," *Harvard Business Review*, December 16, 2015, https://hbr.org/2015/12/executives-protect-your-alone-time.

[76] Newport, *Digital Minimalism*.

[77] "What Silence Makes Possible, " A Quiet Place, March 9, 2015, https://blogs.reed.edu/meditation/2015/03/09/what-silence-makes-possible/.

[78] "Average Unlocks per Day among U.S. Smartphone Users 2018," Statista, accessed May 28, 2024, https://www.statista.com/statistics/1050339/average-unlocks-per-day-us-smartphone-users/.

[79] "44 Smartphone Addiction Statistics for 2024," SlickText, October 28, 2019, https://www.slicktext.com/blog/2019/10/smartphone-addiction-statistics/.

[80] Adrian F. Ward, et al., "Brain Drain: The Mere Presence of One's Own Smartphone Reduces Available Cognitive Capacity," *Journal of the Association for Consumer Research*, 2, no. 2 (April 2017): 140–54, https://doi.org/10.1086/691462.

[81] Gloria Mark, Daniela Gudith, and Ulrich Klocke, "The Cost of Interrupted Work: More Speed and Stress," 2008, 107–10.

[82] Sophie Leroy, "Why Is It so Hard to Do My Work? The Challenge of Attention Residue When Switching between Work Tasks," *Organizational Behavior and Human Decision Processes*, 109, no. 2 (2009): 168–81.

[83] Kim, *Analog Church*.

[84] "More Social Connection Online Tied to Increasing Feelings of Isolation," ScienceDaily, accessed August 6, 2024, https://www.sciencedaily.com/releases/2017/03/170306092742.htm.

[85] Andy Crouch, *The Tech-Wise Family: Everyday Steps for Putting Technology in Its Proper Place* (Baker Books, 2017).

[86] "Your Brain's Ideal Schedule," *Harvard Business Review*, March 26, 2015, https://hbr.org/podcast/2015/03/your-brains-ideal-schedule.

[87] Susan Cunningham, "The Hidden Stress of Cell Phones," UCHealth Today (blog), February 6, 2018, https://www.uchealth.org/today/the-hidden-stress-of-cell-phones/.

Chapter 5

[88] Lewis, *Mere Christianity*.

[89] Douglas Van Steere, *Dimensions of Prayer: Cultivating a Relationship with God* (Upper Room Books, 2002).

[90] "Attention | Etymology of Attention by Etymonline," accessed August 7, 2024, https://www.etymonline.com/word/attention.

[91] John D. Eastwood, et al., "The Unengaged Mind: Defining Boredom in Terms of Attention," *Perspectives on Psychological Science*, 7, no. 5 (2012): 482–95.

[92] Richard P. Feynman, *"Surely You're Joking, Mr. Feynman!": Adventures of a Curious Character* (W. W. Norton & Company, 2010).

[93] Albert Einstein, "It's Not That I'm So Smart, It's Just That I Stay with Problems Longer," The Foundation for a Better Life, accessed August 8, 2024, https://www.passiton.com/inspirational-quotes/5053-albert-einstein.

[94] Mother Teresa, *In the Heart of the World: Thoughts, Stories and Prayers* (New World Library, 1997).

[95] Arnold Bennett, *How to Live on 24 Hours a Day: With The Human Machine*, 1908 (Reprint: Courier Corporation, 2007).

[96] Courtney E. Ackerman, "What Is Kaplan's Attention Restoration Theory (ART)?" PositivePsychology.com, November 13, 2018, https://positivepsychology.com/attention-restoration-theory/.

[97] Gloria Mark, *Attention Span: A Groundbreaking Way to Restore Balance, Happiness and Productivity* (Harlequin, 2023).

[98] Mark, *Attention Span*.

[99] "A Positive Mood Allows Your Brain to Think More Creatively," Association for Psychological Science, accessed August 8, 2024, https://www.psychologicalscience.org/news/releases/a-positive-mood-allows-your-brain-to-think-more-creatively.html.

Chapter 6

[100] Dean Karnazes, *50/50: Secrets I Learned Running 50 Marathons in 50 Days—and How You Too Can Achieve Super Endurance!* (Grand Central Publishing, 2008).

[101] Carr, *The Shallows*.

[102] Carr, *The Shallows*.

[103] "Reading with Algorithms," Post45, accessed August 8, 2024, https://post45.org/sections/contemporaries-essays/reading-with-algorithms/.

[104] Christopher Ingraham, "Leisure reading in the U.S. is at an all-time Low," *Washington Post*, June 29, 2018, https://www.washingtonpost.com/news/wonk/wp/2018/06/29/leisure-reading-in-the-u-s-is-at-an-all-time-low/.

[105] Gallup Inc., "About Half of Americans Reading a Book," Gallup.com, June 3, 2005, https://news.gallup.com/poll/16582/About-Half-Americans-Reading-Book.aspx.

[106] "Book Reading Behavior," American Academy of Arts and Sciences, accessed August 8, 2024, https://www.amacad.org/humanities-indicators/public-life/book-reading-behavior.

[107] Johann Hari, "Are Screens Robbing Us of Our Capacity for Deep Reading?" Literary Hub (blog), January 31, 2022, https://lithub.com/are-screens-robbing-us-of-our-capacity-for-deep-reading/.

[108] Hari, *Stolen Focus*.

[109] "Overview Of Lectio Divina," C. S. Lewis Institute (blog), accessed August 8, 2024, https://www.cslewisinstitute.org/resources/overview-of-lectio-divina/.

[110] "Commonplace Books: A History of Manuscripts and Printed Books from Antiquity to the Twentieth-Century," Museums and Society, April 22, 2024, https://krieger.jhu.edu/museums-society/faculty-books/commonplace-books-a-history-of-manuscripts-and-printed-books-from-antiquity-to-the-twentieth-century/.

[111] "Empathy: College students don't have as much as they used to," University of Michigan News, May 27, 2010, https://news.umich.edu/empathy-college-students-don-t-have-as-much-as-they-used-to/.

[112] *"The iPhone Effect: Social Interactions and a Constant State of 'Poly-Consciousness,'"* The Journalist's Resource (blog), October 20, 2014, https://journalistsresource.org/media/iphone-effect-social-interaction-quality-mobile-device-presence/.

[113] Raymond A. Mar, Keith Oatley, and Jordan B. Peterson, "Exploring the link between reading fiction and empathy: Ruling out individual differences and examining outcomes," De Gruyter, *COMM* 34, no. 4 (December 2009): 407–28, https://doi.org/10.1515/COMM.2009.025.

[114] "7 Scientific Benefits of Reading Printed Books," Mental Floss," August 23, 2018, https://www.mentalfloss.com/article/554845/7-scientific-benefits-reading-printed-books.

Chapter 7

[115] "Folgers® Coffee History, " Folgers®, accessed August 13, 2024, https://www.folgerscoffee.com/history.

[116] "On Folger's Shoulders: Lessons from the Early Years of a Coffee Giant," Covoya, accessed Sept. 24, 2024, https://www.covoyacoffee.com/blog/folgers-coffee-history.html

[117] Theda Radtke, et al., "Digital Detox: An Effective Solution in the Smartphone Era? A Systematic Literature Review," Mobile Media & Communication, 10, no. 2 (May 1, 2022): 190–215, https://doi.org/10.1177/20501579211028647.

[118] Manoush Zomorodi, *Bored and Brilliant: How Spacing out Can Unlock Your Most Productive and Creative Self* (St. Martin's Press, 2017).

[119] Newport, *Digital Minimalism*.

[120] Newport, *Digital Minimalism*.

[121] Aditya Kumar Purohit, Louis Barclay, and Adrian Holzer, "Designing for Digital Detox: Making Social Media Less Addictive with Digital Nudges," 2020, 1–9.

[122] Andrew J. Elliot and Markus A Maier, "Color Psychology: Effects of Perceiving Color on Psychological Functioning in Humans," *Annual Review of Psychology*, 65, no. 1 (2014): 95–120.

Conclusion

[123] Tony Reinke, *God, Technology, and the Christian Life* (Crossway, 2022).

About the Author

Dr. Brian S. Bovee is a seasoned professional in the world of technology, with over two decades of experience shaping how digital tools engage users. Holding a master's and doctorate in information systems, he teaches full-time at California Baptist University, combining cutting-edge research with a deep passion for understanding its impact on our lives. Married since 1995 and living in Southern California, Dr. Bovee enjoys spending time with family, outdoor activities, and anything active when not he is not teaching, writing or doing research.

Read more at www.thefocusedfaith.com.

www.ingramcontent.com/pod-product-compliance
Lightning Source LLC
Chambersburg PA
CBHW060755050426
42449CB00008B/1416